# Corporate Awesome Sauce

## Richie Etwaru

*Leadership Science & Research
by Dhar Ramdehal*

First published by Dog Ear Publishing
4011 Vincennes Rd
Indianapolis, IN 46268
www.dogearpublishing.net

ISBN: 978-1-4575-3417-1

Library of Congress Control Number:    has been applied for

This book is printed on acid-free paper.

Printed in the United States of America

*To my mother Haemdai, thank you from both Mark & I.*

# Corporate Awesome Sauce

I, _____ am

gifting this book to you _____

on the _____ day, of _____, _____. It is my belief and

conviction that this book with help you

_____, _____,

and _____ in your career/life

within the next _____ years.

In return I ask that after reading it and find value, some

time between today and the next five years you pass this book on

to someone else. There is a paragraph below that awaits the half of

a decade ahead.

I, _____ am re-gifting

this book to you _____

on the _____ day, of _____, _____. It is my belief and

conviction that this book with help you

_____, _____,

and _____ in your career/life

within the next _____ years.

This book is not to be re-gifted more than twice,

-Richie

# About the Authors

RICHIE ETWARU

An agent of change, Richie is an infector of thought for which there is no cure. His career has been defined by cognitive jujitsu that places people and companies in powerful positions that drive creativity and success.

He has been a COO for technology at a large financial services company, a divisional CIO at a large investment bank, a co-founder of multiple startups, a Chief Digital Officer of a billion dollar software company, and sits on a few start-up advisory boards.

He is irreverent, unorthodox and skilled in navigating complex organizations yet managing to articulate his vision with focused communication combined with a charismatic style.

DHAR RAMDEHAL

A transformational leader and change agent. Dhar understands change is the only constant in life and for us to evolve, we must transform. His life is defined by challenging the status quo from the lens of change as a manager, colleague, mentor, motivator, facilitator, and leader of transformation.

His experience derives from a wide spectrum of disciplines in leadership, organizational management, business consulting, law, finance, accounting, and taxation. He is skilled in strategic thinking, planning, and execution of organizational initiatives in a constantly evolving world of technology, globalization, and complex organizations changes.

Dhar enjoys sports and music. He is a percussionist and vocalist with expertise in Indian classical, Indian pop, and West Indian genres. He shares this passion with his students at Nirvana Music.

"Edited by Emily Loose"

Emily Loose is an independent editor and publishing consultant. She has worked as a senior acquisitions editor at three of the big five general trade publishing houses, Crown Publishers of Random House, The Penguin Press of Penguin Books, and Free Press of Simon & Schuster, signing and publishing seventeen *New York Times* bestsellers in that time, including books by George Soros, Arianna Huffington, and Ross Douthat, as well as for John Wiley & Sons and the Cambridge University Press. She has specialized in science, history current affairs, popular social science, narrative nonfiction and business. Science books she has edited include Alex Bellos's *Here's Looking at Euclid,* short-listed for the prestigious Samuel Johnson Prize, Nicholas Wade's *Before the Dawn,* which won the National Association of Science Writer's Science in Society award for 2007. She has worked with many academics on award-winning and groudbreaking books, including works by two Noble Prize-winning economists, Douglass North and Elinor Ostrom. She finds great satisfaction in helping researchers write about their work with the clarity and verve that will allow it to reach a wide readership and have optimal impact.

*"There are probably typos in this book."*

# INTRODUCTION

I was born the older of two sons of a couple of schoolteachers in the town of Blairmont, population about 1,000, in Guyana, on the Northern East coast of South America, which is one of the poorest countries of the world. The Guyanese live on a small coastal strip of the country, leaving over 80 percent of the territory untouched rain forest. A land of diversity, in which many cultures have been blended, Guyana is economically poor but is rich in the spirit of hard work.

My parents were no exception. We lived in the countryside, and I grew up feeding chickens, ducks, goats and our one horse. When you live in the countryside of a poor nation like Guyana, you eat what you breed. I found this a great challenge. As a kid when you tend to chickens you name them, at least I did, and they become your friends. As they get older and are laying fewer eggs, you become fearful for them; you know it's inevitable that every cute chicken will eventually become dinner. No matter, every time my parents instructed me to go get a chicken, I went through a great emotional struggle deciding which of my chicken friends would die. Now I can see that this was good training in the demands of survival and the emotional punishment of poverty. It also helped make me keenly aware that I had only one way out; getting good grades in school. Not that my parents would have tolerated anything less.

My fondest memories of my time there are of school. Good grades were my thing. To say I was a nerd would be a complement; I was below the rank of nerd on the social pyramid. An introvert when I was young, I would walk alone to and from school, solemnly, along a mud-caked path. To keep myself busy, I would often pick a rock to kick, and I would kick it all the way there, about two miles. Then, on the way home, I'd pick another rock and kick it all the way back. This might seem the ultimate in pointless uses of time, but the truth is, kicking a single rock such a distance takes skill.

You need a good sense of mass, force, direction, and acceleration. I could have easily lost my rock by kicking it too hard, sending it off into a ditch of water, or into a pile of indistinguishable rocks where it would take cover, or into the bushes along the sides of the path. Even today, when I occasionally see a rock on the sidewalks of New York City, I'll start kicking it around. This damages my shoes and embarrasses my friends, not to mention annoying other pedestrians, but I can't help it; as they say, old habits die hard.

Regardless of the skill involved, whether my father would have looked favorably on my rock kicking is doubtful. He was a stern man, always regaling my younger brother and me with aphorisms like "the most limited resource in the world is time." When we misbehaved, he would berate my mom with "what you tolerate is what you will get."

My parents were polar opposites when it came to us; while he ruled with an iron fist, she wore the velvet glove. And where my mother taught us about the importance of family, compassion toward others, and wining with grace, my father stressed excellence. His favorite line was from George Orwell's *Animal Farm*, "all men are created equal, some are just more equal than others." He seemed not to have appreciated that Orwell was being satirical, or chose not to.

Though I became distanced from my father after he and my mother divorced, I'm grateful for the lessons he taught me about hard work, and for how he helped instill in me a determination not to be under anyone's thumb. Orwell directed his satire in *Animal Farm* at the brutality and hypocrisy of the Soviet system, but he might well have written a sequel set in the corporate world. I've encountered plenty of characters that could have come straight out of Orwell in my career. I'm sure you have, or will, too. Which is why it's so important to know the recipe for corporate awesome sauce.

I decided to write this book after I realized one day that for years I'd been lying to people when students, friends and colleagues asked me what I thought were the secrets to success.

Some time around 2009, UBS decided to appoint me to its Graduate Trainee Program (GTP) Director's Council, a group of Directors and higher-ups at the firm who travel to top colleges around the country and meet with students one on one as well as making presentations about the pros and cons of working in financial services. A key function is to spot the best graduating students and bring them into the firm.

I turned out to be good at the work because I spoke the language of Millennials and I looked much younger than my age, so the students connected with me. I also seem to have had a knack for picking the right talent, as three of the five students I brought into the firm during 2009 and 2010 went on to be promoted early, ahead of their peers. They were so talented that I made sure to steal them from their managers when I needed their smarts and creativity for projects (ingredient 4 of awesome sauce; more on that later).

But I realized one night that I had been giving the students I met with absolutely the wrong advice. I had made a presentation at Pennsylvania State University to two dozen bright minds about the merits of working in financial services and the pros and cons of joining UBS, and afterward I did something I should not have done; I agreed to go out for drinks with a group of them, for which I not only paid quite a hefty financial tab (after all, they were college students) but paid dearly physically the next morning interviewing students with a horrible hangover. That wasn't the main lesson I learned from that night though.

On the way back home from the bar that morning at about 2 a.m. a bright, still completely coherent young lad asked me "Richie if you could tell me three things that you used to get where you are fast, what would they be?" A great question. I told him to find good mentors, to do work he is passionate about, and to take only calculated risks. He seemed excited by the advice, but for whatever reason, maybe because he seemed like such a good guy, I suddenly realized what I had told him wasn't true. It was simply affirmation of advice he'd probably heard many times before, and what he and others expected to hear. Those were not the ways I'd gotten ahead.

I didn't seek mentors, though I believe in mentoring. The truth is, though, that I learned much more from mentoring than from being mentored. I didn't follow one deep passion; I change what I am passionate about daily. And taking risks I haven't calculated is my core modus operandi. I had been lying.

On the drive home from the trip, I wrestled with trying to pinpoint when it was that I had started to lie in giving this advice, and what made me lie. I began to wonder, how many people had I lied to??? I had a four-hour drive ahead of me, and in part to stop from falling asleep, I decided to start making calls. I called colleagues I remembered had asked me about success secrets; I called people I had mentored, old business partners, and a few close friends. I asked them all, "What advice did I give you for success?" All of them responded, "You said to find good mentors, do work you're passionate about, and take only calculated risks." I was appalled, and ashamed. I estimated that I had given over a thousand people this advice in those supposedly more candid, one-on-one conversations after conferences, at career fairs, at work, and while waiting for flights at the airport. I'd given them advice that was worthless to me and the opposite of what I actually did.

Not long after that I finished my stint on the GTP Director's Council, and I didn't give the realization much more thought. But then, about a year later in 2011, I visited my cousin, Dhar Ramdehal, in Orlando. Dhar had moved to the U.S. from Guyana as a child some thirty years prior and was starting his Ph.D. in leadership studies at a university there while also pursuing his lifelong passion for music by teaching at a music school. He had told his students about me and he said that they wanted me to come talk to them about how to get ahead. I walked into the music school a few days later feeling dread that I was about to lie once again.

Dhar's classroom was alive in controlled chaos. He was teaching Indian classical music that day, and while one child played an Indian drum called a tabla in one corner, a small group of students sang in another part of the room, others were hunched over their instruments practicing on their own. Instruments, books and Apple Mac Airs were strewn all around the floor, and the walls were filled with pictures of students performing and of traditional Indian dancers and musicians. The effect was of a joyful exuberance, but as I walked in, an awkward silence took over the room. Some of the students stared at me and seemed to be thinking, "You're interrupting our music so this had better be good." Others kept fiddling with their instruments or typing on their laptops.

All of the color of the room seemed to fade into dull black and white, and I realized that after having spoken to groups in the thousands before of though-minded professionals, I'd never felt quite this level of demand to hear something valuable.

I found myself telling them the unvarnished truth; it just poured out. I told them that the fear of being fired is one of the largest obstacles to success, and that it's important to try to get fired. I told them that being able to draw was more important than being able to write, and that business is more about friendships than about political favors. I told them that most of the people who work for you will not be top talent and you have to learn how to steal top talent. And I told them that you must give success to others willingly and openly and that it will come back around to you every time. The more I said, the more closely they listened. Laptops were closed, instruments were set aside. I had gotten their full attention, and I saw on their faces nothing like the look of affirmation I had seen with the student that morning at 2a.m at Pennsylvania State University. I saw surprise and relief, recognition that I was giving them the straight scoop.

That night back at Dhar's house, as we sat on his balcony overlooking a pond in the back yard talking and looking for alligators, which we always do for hours when I visit him (we never spot any – I am an alligator repellant – but invariably Dhar sees one a few days after I leave and snaps a picture to send me), Dhar asked me "Why didn't you ever give me that advice?"

I had even lied to him.

It was then that the reason I had lied to so many dawned on me. Most of those who had asked me what I had done to accelerate my success were either my age or older, like Dhar; I had only recently begun talking to students and co-workers from the Millennial and Generation Y cohorts. I realized that if I had given those older than the Millennials the advice I'd given at the music school earlier that day, the older folks would have laughed at me, or at least would not have been convinced, and decided I had a screw loose. But those kids in the school, I could see, thought differently.

Much has been written about how the Millennials struggle with the traditional rules of the corporate world, and I think this is because they know that those rules — get good mentors, work on what you are passionate about, and take only calculate risks, blah blah blah —

don't work. Following the old rules feels to them like playing into the trap of an outmoded system and they are seeking a better way. Everybody should be seeking the same, because it's true that the old rules don't work anymore, if they ever really did.

It was when I started to ignore the rules that my whole attitude about work, and success, changed. I began to truly love my work life, and I took on all kinds of new challenges, made all kinds of change happen, and made enough money, while getting lots of promotions too. But I hadn't really appreciated that until my visit with Dhar.

When I got home from my visit to Orlando, I decided to dig systematically into what I'd actually done that had led to my success despite breaking the rules and repeatedly almost getting fired. I thought back through the years and interviewed many of those I'd worked with. At the same time I began reading widely in the literature about success, from psychology and behavioral science to the research on business leadership and management, to probe into why the decidedly unconventional approach I'd taken had worked. I read biographies of great business leaders, loads of *Harvard Business Review* articles, leading gurus of success like Robert Kiyoski and Guy Kawaswaki, and watched hours and hours of videos of speeches on the topic, from notable commencement addresses to the latest TED talks.

I realized I'd become more successful not despite almost being fired many times, but in large part because of that. I discovered the recipe for what I call corporate awesome sauce; the recipe that will set you apart, make you memorable, and allow you to leap tall buildings, subvert stupid procedures, spend little to no time in mind-numbing meetings, and put your ideas into rapid action.

Mind you, there may be other recipes for awesome sauce; any good sauce is bound to have its variations. My recipe has twelve ingredients; twelve key practices I realized had made all the difference in me becoming happier with my work and feeling on a daily basis that I was thriving. They are all about how to buck the maddening inanities of corporate rules and politics and be recognized as someone who thinks differently and has creative ideas that solve problems. In this book, I'm going to share my recipe with you.

The book is aimed at those who:

- are just starting your career
- those who are stuck in the middle ranks of an organization and want to break out to higher ground
- those who want out of your current work but don't know where you want to go or how to get there
- those who are almost at the top, but always find yourself working for a moron, and
- those who have done everything right, but find that someone less impressive always seems to beat you out of promotions and accolades.

In short, I've written the book for just about every person in corporate life.

The fact is that most people who work in the corporate world will be in one of these five situations at one point or another, and often they'll go through all of them. For the first fifteen years of my career, I found myself in one or another of them over and over.

I certainly haven't managed to evade all of the aggravations – that would be impossible –but I deal with them in a completely different way than I did at the start of my career. I've learned to love that I am never out and never really in, and that I am always close to being fired. I cherish making new starts and being at the bottom of the ladder again. I've learned to love being in the middle of organizations, because it's the most fun, with the most opportunity to make change happen. I've learned to make it my business to let others take credit and get ahead. I've even learned to like working under morons, because I look good making them look good. I hope this book will help you spice up your work life and have as much fun in the corporate world as I've learned to. Oh, and achieve success, too, of course. All of the stories I tell are true, but I've shortened them to get right to the point. So, on that note, please dig in.

*While writing this chapter, I listened to*
*Redemption Song by Bob Marley*

# INGREDIENT 1

## Come close to being fired on a monthly basis

My good friend Ray Wang from Constellation Research will tell you "Since 2000, 52 percent of the companies in the Fortune 500 have either gone bankrupt, been acquired, ceased to exist, or dropped out of the Fortune 500. In fact, the pace of change has increased, competition has intensified, and business models have been disrupted. Digitization of business is a key factor in this accelerated pace of change. Information flows faster." I like the way Ray makes his point clearly and powerfully; the pace of change itself is changing. Any organization standing still will soon be dead.

Being able to change – and I'm not talking about only in incremental ways, but often in more dramatic ones — is important for all of us at the personal level as well as for organizations. In order to make good new things happen, you must be able to change yourself, change your team, your department, your organization, and maybe even your industry. And to do that, you must overcome the single biggest obstacle to change: the fear of being fired/Failure.

Almost all employees of organizations, top and bottom, shy away from taking the kind of risks that lead to innovations that really make a difference because we feel dependent on a reliable paycheck, and are horrified by the stigma of being booted. This means that we often contort ourselves into bundles of contradictions about what we really think should be done, holding us back from standing out and making real change happen.

Is being fired really that bad?

Courtesy of Business Insider, here is a list of famous successful folks who thrived after being fired:

* Steve Jobs, who was fired from Apple.
* Walt Disney, who was fired from the Kansas City Star because his editor thought he lacked imagination.
* Mark Cuban was from fired from his job as a computer store sales person.
* J.K. Rowling was fired from her job as a secretary at Amnesty International.
* Michael Bloomberg was let go from Solomon Brothers when it was sold to the banking conglomerate now known as Citigroup.
* Anna Wintour was fired after only nine months at *Harper's Bazaar*.
* Madonna was fired from her job at the Dunkin Donuts then in Times Square.
* Oprah Winfrey was fired by a Baltimore news producer who told her she was "unfit for television news."
* Jerry Seinfeld was fired from his role on the show Benson after only three episodes had been shot.
* Robert Redford was fired from a low-level, unskilled job at Standard Oil.
* One of the most respected coaches in football, Bill Belichick, was fired by the Cleveland Browns.
* Lee Iacocca, who achieved national icon status as the man who saved Chrysler, was fired from his job as CEO of Ford.

Yet, we are all afraid of being fired.

I practice coming close to being fired once a month, though I suggest that for a start you give it a go once per year, then once per quarter, until you get really good at it.

Of course, it would be easy to actually *get* fired, which can be done by all sorts of unproductive means; rank insubordination, laziness, embezzlement. What you want to be doing, instead, is finding the sweet spot in which you're pushing the envelope, raising all kinds of hackles — even often screams of protest — all for good reason. And knowing when you should do so is really quite simple: when you can think of a change your organization should be making, and you also can immediately think of the person who will say no, you've got it!

So here is a rule: if you can't think of that first person who will say no, don't even bother with the idea. It's not good enough to spend any time, or personal capital, on. However, when you know right away who the naysayer, or multiple naysayers, will be go for it, and try as hard as you can to get fired.

That may sound extreme, but the truth is that once I found myself operating this way – which wasn't so much a conscious choice as an irresistible urge — all kinds of good things followed. Whenever I found myself pressing on, even though I'd pissed off my boss, his boss, my whole department or another department, I'd find myself thinking, "What is the worst that can happen? They will fire me." I had realized that I'd rather be fired than be a yes man, and it's been the single best thing for my career.

Now I should be quick to say that this lack of fear I felt about being fired came from being fired. That wasn't due to an idea I was pushing for, it was because some years earlier I had been charged with Driving While Intoxicated and I hadn't explicitly disclosed that to my employer. That's not to say that I hadn't been pushing hard for changes; I had been tormenting my managers for months. But here's the thing. When HR suggested I be let go, I expected all of those company leaders I'd been driving crazy would be glad to see me go. The opposite happened. They pulled out the stops to save me.

I got fired anyway, because I told the HR and compliance folks to go screw themselves (it was time to go.) But the support I got from the people I'd given such hell to made me realize that *good ideas that strain organizations do not get you fired.* (Also note, telling HR and compliance to screw themselves *does.*) On the contrary, they get you noticed. Sometimes, they even get you promoted, and sometimes they get you promoted *fast.*

## Practice ugly honesty, or, if you are going to be on stage, be of value

The most annoying thing about trade shows or conferences, among many, is that no one ever tells the real story on stage. Speakers at conferences are generally either on the buy side, meaning the ones buying from the vendors, or they are the vendors on the sell side. The conference organizers may throw in a pundit or a comedian for the after dinner treat, but mostly you are dealing with buy side and sell side folks.

Those on the buy side cannot really disclose the state of the art because their speeches are severely sanitized by the corporate communications and compliance groups of organizations that buy. Basically if you are senior enough to know something meaningful in an organization that buys from vendors, when you go out to speak you are presenting the least you possibly can. Meanwhile, the vendors on the sell side are so starved for stage time to hawk their wares that their entire time on stage is a sales pitch. So, yes, I'm saying there is really no value in going to conventional tradeshows or conferences.

But it's just about impossible to get out of going to all of them. So there I was one day, speaking at a trade show while working on the buy side, for UBS as a Director, managing the applied innovation portfolio. I had decided to deliver the ugly truth of the business:

- That even when it might be possible for technology and innovation to thrive, it doesn't.
- That leaders making decisions on large software purchases do not make their decisions on the basis of making their teams better, faster or smaller. Most of the time it's the friendliness of the sales person and the amount of dinners and bottles of wine he's lavished on the purchaser that makes the decision.
- For the most part, if you know enough about business software, you know that all business software is equal; some is just more equal than others.

Half of the crowd suspected I was mentally unfit, and the other half was sure I was.

Nonetheless I was invited to a few dinners afterwards. I accepted one of the invites, from a CEO whose company was selling, wait for it, "a future state mobility platform for large enterprises to take their past information and technology investments and 'white label' them onto the mobile channel". Translation: they had an invention that could deliver all of a company's technology on Apple iPads without hiring any developers, and letting all of the developers that built the desktop technology go.

Over dinner with a number of people from his team the CEO asked me, "How do you get away with telling the truth?" I told him, "I never ask permission from my communications or compliance teams; I believe I have enough common sense to know what to say and what not to." We were in San Francisco and he jokingly responded that we were in the "passive aggressive capital of the world," and told me how much he appreciated that I was blunt and to the point. He also warned me, "That is going to get you fired eventually," and I responded "Yes, or close; I'm trying to come close to being fired once a month."

During the rest of dinner we continued with brutal nonesty. I learned a lot about his business, and he learned quite a bit about the design of the decision process of enterprises buying technology from vendors. One of the people on his team commented that it was the most honest conversation they'd experienced having with him. Remember, I had met him just two hours prior. We formed such a good bond that we stayed in touch and became good friends.

There is power in being direct and factual. If you fear being fired, it impedes your ability to be direct and factual.

## When my boss thought I must be slacking off

One of the smartest guys I've ever worked for was my boss at UBS, Tony Pizi. When I first started working for him, he called me into his office and he plotted a bell curve on his white board. Turning to me, he said, "You're in the top five percent of the curve, aren't you?" I denied it, but he called me on my denial and said, "Everyone who works for me is likely in that top five percent. Your job is to figure out where you are on a bell curve of that top five percent. I'll see you again in a month."

Before long, he realized that I was what a good friend of mine calls an infector. My friend said to me one day, "You're an infector, you spread infections that make companies healthy." Tony decided that my job would be to strain the status quo, infecting others to join the cause.

One month (we worked so well we only met monthly), he said to me, "You must be slacking off." I responded "WTF?" He laughed and said, "I didn't get any complaints this month from anyone senior that I should fire you." I had been leading a companywide project to install an IT capability around the company that would enable us to exchange data with all partners and competitors quickly and without any compliance risk. Just imagine the push back I was getting from the technology architecture folks, the risk and compliance folks, the privacy people and the general technology staff.

But Tony and I knew we needed to become a company that used data from all sources possible to help our clients, and we had to do it without putting our clients, ourselves or our shareholders at risk. The kicker was that I had to get it done in 90 days, because we had a large partner who needed such data exchange by that time. During the three months, I tried and tried and tried to get fired, breaking down one wall at a time, and Tony got lots of complaints the first two months. But then, in the last 30 days, he got not a single one.

I had infected people, one by one.

A particularly hard case was a naysayer in privacy. He told me I was insane to attempt such a project in 90 days, and he was gunning for me hard. I called him one day and said "whether I do this or not, eventually enterprises will be more information friendly, do you want to be the guy who defends old history, or the guy seen as the patron saint for the firm because he was on the right side of history?" Months later the same naysayer told me he'd come onboard because he "didn't want to be on the wrong side of history".

I tell this story to illustrate that when you're an infector, you've got to expect that some people really will want to see you fired. Every time I've infected change, I've known who the naysayers would be. And once you know who the naysayer is/will be, what you are telling yourself is you know enough about this to go for it.

You simply have to be prepared to piss people off.

The key questions to keep in mind are, Who? And how many at once? You have to be able to find the right balance between being a tough change enforcer and a politician. Here are three quick tips.

1. Think like the CEO – you must learn what the CEO cares about. If you are not high enough in the organization to speak with the CEO, carefully read the messages he or she sends to employees, investors and customers. Go to town halls, watch corporate videos, and pay close attention to his or her remarks in the press. Thinking like the CEO will help you know how hard to push and when to compromise.

2. Learn the organization chart and know the biases, goals and breaking points of every individual you must deal with in the organization. When you go into a meeting, you must know how every person's upward reporting structure looks, all the way up to the CEO. Each "vertical function" — compliance, operations, marketing, technology, or sales — has its own goals and biases, as well as grudges against others. Understanding the power structure and where the fault lines are enables you to be strategic about whom to lobby for what when.

3. Study the culture of the organization like an ethnographer. At Lehman brothers, I learned very quickly that decisions were made around 7:30 am in the morning in the executive halls. If you were not there in the mix, you would simply hear about them later. All organizations have nuances about how decisions are made and ideas are explored. At Cegedim where I work at this writing, decisions are made by consensus, so you want to make sure you "pre-sell" an idea to all committee members before you bring it to the full committee.

The role of the agitator, the disruptor; the guy/gal who always says what others are thinking but keeping quiet about; the person who does exactly what he/she was told not to do and makes it work really does exist in organizations. One of my favorite examples is Paul Bucheit, the guy at Google who was tasked with creating Gmail. Those involved in the development of the service were divided about whether or not ads should be served to Gmail users. Bucheit wanted to serve ads so that Gmail could pay for itself and users could have a great deal more storage space, but others feared ads would creep Gmail users out and be seen as an invasion of privacy. One night Marisa Mayer, then an executive at Google overseeing the development of many products, and Bucheit were discussing the issue, and when Mayer left the office late that night, she said to Bucheit, "So, Paul, we agreed, we're not exploring the whole ad thing right now?" He agreed. But then, during the rest of the night, he proceeded to build a prototype of Gmail with ads. The next morning, when Larry Page and Sergey Brin logged into their Gmail accounts, they loved it. So Gmail has ads, and users have a crazy amount of storage space. This is what I mean by trying to get fired. Playing this role is exhilarating, largely because you know you're driving value.

Of course getting fired isn't the goal, but you're not going to know that you're being disruptive enough to really make change happen if you're not hearing regularly that you're coming close to being fired; not as a constant condition (that probably means you're about to be fired), but pretty often.

Succeeding at this takes three key requirements. First, you have to reject the fundamental principle we all learn early that having a job is a good thing and being fired is a bad thing. Sometimes being out of a job is the only way you find a much better opportunity. If you're talented, you didn't want to work there anyway; your boss or the company was going to hold you back. You're either going to find a new job or make one for yourself. You have to believe that.

Lee Iacocca is a good example. He had risen up the ranks at Ford from success to success, but once at the top, he found himself at loggerheads with Henry Ford II. Rather than buckling to Ford's will, he got himself fired. Which worked out quite well for him, as he went on to become something of an American folk hero by turning around Chrysler.

The second requirement is that you have to know how to choose your battles. Here are some key tips for doing so:

* Always think about why the change has not been made before.
* Carefully consider whether what you are attempting to do can be categorized as common sense; the more it can, the better the opportunity.
* Look at your company's competitors to see if they are attacking the problem or not.
* Discover whether other companies have failed because they did not do what you are recommending. If you cannot find examples, carefully reconsider whether the change is essential.
* Make a friend in legal and compliance and learn the regulations of your industry, company and department. You may discover that the change you want to make has simply too big a hurdle to clear.
* Ask yourself what the CEO would think if he or she found out what you are pushing for.

Finally, you have to lose your fear.

# Fear Itself  –

In his first inaugural address, Franklin Roosevelt famously said to the American people, who had been staring into the abyss of the Great Depression, "the only thing we have to fear is fear itself."

Fear is a powerful emotion; its hold on us should never to be underestimated. Our brains have evolved through the millennia to shut our logical faculties down in the face of danger. Thinking logically takes too much time and energy. Our rational forebrain, with its carefully calibrated assessment of risk, is bullied into submission by the emotional and impulsive animal brain. Risks are exaggerated. With every step we see a snake in the grass. Our eyes become fixated on the danger right before us and we lose sight of the bigger picture and the longer term.

One of the most potent fears is the fear of change. It's in part a fear of the unknown. So often, we'll choose the devil we know over the uncertainty of what other, more horrible monster we might end up with. (We know how to eek out a decent profit. Whereas with a whole new product line…) It's also a fear of conflict. We know that because the fear of change is so pervasive, we'll inevitably face rearguard actions, and often outright subterfuge. And finally, it's the fear of failure. What if we f..ck things up? What if the change we have made such a fuss about all goes horribly wrong?

Which brings us to the most insidious fear of all in corporate life; the fear of being fired. It's one of those especially insidious fears, like that of tarantulas, that seem perfectly rational.

Why did Donald Trump use the phrase, "you are fired?" Because just the word "fired" has such a powerful impact. It's origins are said, by some accounts, to be in an old ritual of banishment. The term might come from a practice in old time of the limestone miners in the Mendip Mountains, in the southwest of England. It's said that if a miner was caught stealing from the mine, his fellow miners would burn his house down, forcing him from the mining community. Some accounts say they would do so with him in it.

An interesting account of a more recent origin has it that John Henry Patterson,  the founder of the NCR Cash Register Company, who is reputed to have been one nasty and tough taskmaster, let one of his employees  go by ordering his desk to be taken onto the company's lawn and set on fire.   Still another explanation is that it's derived from firing a gun, so, metaphorically, you're killing an employee off.

Whatever the true origin, the term fits the fear, and we have many good reasons to be afraid. Abraham Maslov's famous pyramid of human needs rises from a base of the fundamentals of survival — food, shelter and warmth and safety — up to psychological needs such as freedom from fear, self-esteem and confidence, and finally the need for self-actualization. All of these seem clearly threatened by being fired.

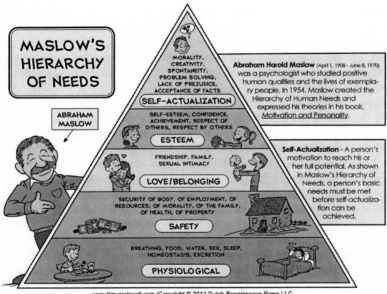

MASLOW'S HIERARCHY OF NEEDS

ABRAHAM MASLOW

**SELF-ACTUALIZATION** — MORALITY, CREATIVITY, SPONTANEITY, PROBLEM SOLVING, LACK OF PREJUDICE, ACCEPTANCE OF FACTS

**ESTEEM** — SELF-ESTEEM, CONFIDENCE, ACHIEVEMENT, RESPECT OF OTHERS, RESPECT BY OTHERS

**LOVE/BELONGING** — FRIENDSHIP, FAMILY, SEXUAL INTIMACY

**SAFETY** — SECURITY OF BODY, OF EMPLOYMENT, OF RESOURCES, OF MORALITY, OF THE FAMILY, OF HEALTH, OF PROPERTY

**PHYSIOLOGICAL** — BREATHING, FOOD, WATER, SEX, SLEEP, HOMEOSTASIS, EXCRETION

**Abraham Harold Maslow** (April 1, 1908 - June 8, 1970) was a psychologist who studied positive human qualities and the lives of exemplary people. In 1954, Maslow created the Hierarchy of Human Needs and expressed his theories in his book, Motivation and Personality.

**Self-Actualization** - A person's motivation to reach his or her full potential. As shown in Maslow's Hierarchy of Needs, a person's basic needs must be met before self-actualization can be achieved.

www.timvandevall.com |Copyright © 2013 Dutch Renaissance Press LLC.

No question, the effects can be pernicious. Researchers have shown that being fired can cause not only serious psychological distress, such as anxiety and depression, but also can have physical effects, such as an increase in blood pressure and hypertension.

So I'm not saying that there's no reason for the fear of being fired. I'm saying that this is why freeing yourself from the fear is so liberating, and also that this is why you have to add in all of the other ingredients to your corporate awesome sauce.

Trying to get fired every month or so on its own is only a recipe for being fired. As a part of awesome sauce, it frees up your creativity and dials up your courage to speak up. It lets your colleagues and managers know that you're an innovation generator who has talent for creative destruction and disruption. And even the most hidebound corporations have begun to understand that they need people who aren't afraid to be disruptive, who can be counted on to challenge the status quo, and will roll their eyes at whatever brilliant power points consultants have so lavishly, and lucratively, crafted.

Times have changed, and organizations are in desperate need of divergent thinking to catalyze innovation. Evolve or die is the Darwinian creed, and it's never been truer for businesses than now.

Of course disruption has always been a threat to even the most successful businesses. Woolworths, RCA, Polaroid, E.F. Hutton, General Foods, Circuit City; all were market leaders at one point and failed. Many failed companies still had plenty of loyal customers when they went under. Consider once mighty Pan American World Airways, which was one of the oldest and for a time most successful airlines. The brand still has such luster that a TV show about Pan Am stewardesses and pilots was put on the air a few years ago (though that, too, failed) and there are numerous luggage lines that offer retro Pan Am travel bags with the company's famous logo.

But failures today are faster.

Consider the torturous last few years for Blackberry, once such a trailblazer in the smart phone market. Game maker Zynga was all the rage only a couple of years ago and is now desperately struggling. Abercrombie & Fitch has gone in the last few years from the booming, newly hip brand for teens to a stock dive of 30 percent in the last year. The stakes could not be higher, and the solution is innovative thinking and the willingness to take risks. Those who establish a track record for being bold and catalyzing good change are more valuable than ever.

Another distinct advantage of losing your fear is that in its absence, the frontal cortex is rather intelligent at analyzing and assessing risk. The more you are able to work with your forebrain, the less you are focused on immediate concerns and the better you can gain a longer-term and wider-angle perspective on the risks your company is facing down the road and the changes you should be pushing for. The more you become known for having a skill for seeing the road ahead and how to navigate it successfully, the more awesome your sauce will be.

So many people in corporate life are focused on doing the right things, but ask yourself, what are the right things to do? And how long will they be the right things to do instead of a new set of things you'd better start doing?

It's been widely reported that when the great hockey player Wayne Gretzsky was asked, "Why do you always find the puck?" he replied, "I am never where the puck is, but where the puck is going to be." " But Wayne never actually said that. The truth is, as explained in a great article in *Fast Company*, Gretsky's dad once told a pee wee hockey team he was coaching, "Go to where the puck is going, not where it has been." Nevertheless, Wayne may as well have said it since that was the way he played.

You want to always be keeping your eye on where the puck is going and skating with all your energy to it, now more than ever, with the speed of change so ramped up. Sometimes that will mean someone will blindside you; sometimes it will mean skating too fast and crashing into the boards. But if you're not prepared to take those hits, you're never going to be a Wayne Gretsky.

Disruptive innovation isn't a matter of corporate strategy; it's a matter of disruptive individuals.

So lose your fear and start trying to get fired!

*While writing this chapter, I listened to*
*Billy Jean by Michael Jackson*

# INGREDIENT 2

## *Tell stories, and don't be afraid to be funny*

Making change happen is mostly about what I call "trading influence." Influence as a noun is described as the capacity to have an effect on the character, development, or behavior of someone or something, or as the actual effect itself. I prefer to think of influence is the raw material of change; the means of making change happen, one human at a time.

In order to influence others, you have to learn to be a leader, but you can't be a leader without instilling a sense of fellowship among those on your team. After all, if you are a leader and no one is following you, you're really just a guy or gal walking alone.

The primary means of building that fellowship, and getting buy-in for your ideas, is communication. But let's face it, these days we're all just about maxed out on so much communication: constant phone calls, emails, texts, social media posts, videoconferences, not to mention the time suck of face to face meetings (during which so many of us are getting texts, emails, and social media posts).

The philosopher of communication Marshall Mcluhan famously wrote in his 1964 book *Understanding Media* "the medium is the message." He was pointing to the new power of television over our lives, and he was saying that the technology with which a message was being delivered had become at least as influential over us as the content of the message, if not more. Email, cell phone calls, texts, social media, video and even meeting rooms are all mediums. It's time for us to realize they all have too much power over us and that, no, the message is *not* the medium, and the message matters more than the medium, much more.

The great irony of the flood of communication today is that so often we're not really communicating with it. People are overwhelmed. Most of the time when we're communicating these days, we're just transacting. We're not making people think; we're not getting them to sit up and really listen; we're not stimulating their imaginations and getting their creative juices flowing; and we're not making a lasting impression on them and effectively influencing them.

Consider just this one fact: power point has become the de facto conference presentation medium, and one research study showed that people tend to remember the content of only four out of twenty slides after just a couple of days.

Now, go and watch the TED talk by creativity expert Ken Robinson, "How Schools Kill Creativity," which has been viewed over 26 million times. I'm hoping you haven't known who Ken Robinson is before, because after you watch his talk, you will find that you will not be able to forget him. Why? Because he's one of the funniest people and best storytellers on the planet.

## A story is worth a thousand pictures

The best way to develop followers and to exercise influence is to tell stories. Well, to tell good stories.

A great deal of research has illuminated just how powerful the telling of a good story is, and why. While our brains evolved to be hyper-alert to danger, they also evolved to pay very close attention to stories. No wonder scary stories are so popular! In fact, it's thought that some of the earliest known remains of human communication, the ancient cave paintings of France and Spain, with their stunning images of large horned animals and lion and tiger-like predators, were created in part to tell stories about the dangers to watch out for while hunting.

Brain science has shown that stories ignite our brains much more fully than being lectured to – or shown a power point. If we're lectured to, only the parts of the brain that are involved in processing language are activated, but when we're told a story, all of the parts of the brain that would be activated if we actually experienced the events of the story are activated. It's like we really are living the experience in our brains. And on top of that, research has shown that the brains of the storyteller and the listener become synchronized, a phenomenon known as "neural coupling." The areas of the storyteller's brain that are activated as she tells the story are also activated in her listeners. Talk about building fellowship.

But probably the most powerful thing about stories is that if you tell them right, people remember them. Two researchers at Yale have argued that stories about our experiences are actually the "fundamental constituents" of human memory. Studies have shown that people recall information better if it is presented to them in a narrative style. And stories are also more persuasive. For example, one study showed that legal arguments are more convincing if they're made by telling a story.

So you gain more mindshare with any audience, whether one on one or up on a big conference stage, when you tell stories; but remember, they've got to be good ones.

## I built my first cloud at the age of seven

The first time I met the COO of UBS Wealth Management, she told me she was impressed by some cool regiggling of the flux capacitor in a piece of enterprise software my team had developed, with BrightIdeas. (Don't worry about what a flux capacitor is; I mention it just because it sounds cool, which is always good for a story.) After that, we built a working relationship, and one day over a scheduled cup of coffee she asked me "what is it that makes you break things down and re-assemble them over and over, and why is it that when you find something cool you can't wait to tell others about it?" (Like the flux capacitor.)

I hadn't known I did these things! But immediately, I realized, she was right. I had started breaking things down and sharing cool things in my early childhood. I found myself telling her a story.

You see, when I was six my parents bought me a one hundred piece puzzle, and at first it was a blast to fix because it was so challenging, but as you would expect, after I'd assembled it a few times, I became bored by it. Like any kid, I begged for a second puzzle, and then I quickly became bored with that too. Of course I petitioned for a third, but my parents wisely suggested that instead I try to find a way to have more fun with the two puzzles I already had.

That was when I figured out that I could put the pieces of the two puzzles I had in a bag and shake them all up and then try to assemble the puzzles from the more confusing jumble. That was fun for a while. But then I realized that I could have even more fun if I assembled the puzzles picture side down, onto pieces of cardboard, and then drew my own pictures on the back of them, my own pictures would be challenging to assemble.

Then, after I'd turned seven, I realized that I could vastly multiply the fun. I could start a network of other kids who had puzzles they were bored with and create a puzzle exchange program. Remember that I grew up in rural Guyana, the second poorest country in the world. I didn't have anything like eBay, but I created my own puzzle cloud network, with just a bicycle, a few plastic bags for collecting the puzzle pieces, a notebook, and a pencil.

It wasn't long after I'd told her that story that she asked me to lead innovation at the firm. Suddenly I was Director of Innovation of a work unit called the Transformation Group! The story didn't get me the job – I had good credentials and a track record of innovation — but I'm sure that it improved my odds of being picked. So many others at the company were as well qualified as I was; but this simple story made me stand out. And to this day, whenever that COO introduces me to people, she has me tell them the story. I've even had people I told the story tell me later that they told it to their kids.

You can't influence anyone unless they remember you. You can't make them remember you (except in a bad way) if you bore them.

## Why 5:05 p.m. sucks

A little over three years ago, I was asked to deliver a speech on how big data will change the world and how companies can learn to take advantage of it. I talked about how the volume of data is not what's most important, but rather its veracity – there is so much bad data – and the intelligence and creativity with which we analyze it. To illustrate my points, I discussed how healthcare will be changed when we realize that the human body is the world's largest database.

I started with a story, as I always do. As research leading up to my speech, I told them, I had started using an electronic device (I used a Lark, this was way before the fitbit) to monitor my heartbeat and my sleep patterns, one of the fruitful new types of "big data" analysis. When I had about six months of 24/7 heart rate data and nightly sleep data I went for my once every five years check up (as every geek does), and after the doctor had checked my vitals, he told me I was okay. I asked him, "How is my heart?" and he said "fine, I checked it." It was then I told them, "that I whipped out my own heart data, and proceeded to point out to him how poor his single point in time measure was." Blah, blah …. I could see they weren't engaged. This was only an okay story; not a good enough story!

So I then told them another story. I had noticed in my heart data that around 5:05 p.m. every Monday through Thursday, but not on Friday or the weekends, the rate of my heartbeat would spike up a little, becoming about 3% to 5% faster. I could see this created some intrigue; the crowd was perking up. Always try to create intrigue; it's one of the best techniques of good storytelling. I then shared that I formulated a hypothesis about what was causing the spikes, and that I decided to test it. So I hacked my phone and logged every text and call I received or placed and to whom, and then correlated that with my heartbeat data. Ah hah! My hypothesis was right!

If you work in a typical non-exempt corporate job – in which you're not paid overtime and your hours are insane —and your significant other has a job with more fixed hours, I told them, you may have experienced this. My girlfriend is a healthcare provider, and her day finishes at 5:00 p.m. sharp, every Monday through Thursday. Now I could see they were really loving this story. I told them that like clockwork, every Monday through Thursday between around 5:05 to 5:15 she calls or texts me to ask when I'll be leaving the office. Of course, I never really know, I said. I might be just about ready to leave, or maybe in 30 minutes, or I might get caught up in something and not be done for several hours. For most of us in corporate jobs it depends on how we're feeling, how creative we can get with our prioritization and delegation, and how important the thing/activity other than work we want to do is. I could see they were relating to that. Then I went for the finish. "So almost every Monday through Thursday between 5:05 pm and 5:15 p.m. I tell my girlfriend I'm not sure when I'll be leaving the office, and it frustrates me as much as it frustrates her! This is what was causing my heartbeat to spike by 3% - 5%."

The story really drove the point home about how being creative about the ways we dig into all the data we're gathering is the key.

Fast-forward three years, and I am at another conference. The CIO of a pharmaceutical manufacturing company comes up to me and asks "so did you marry her?" It turned out that he was in the audience that day and when he saw me, he right away remembered the story. We had a good laugh about it, and after that, we kept in touch. Today, he is one of my key connections in the pharmaceutical industry as I make my way into work in the field. I need all the help I can get as I help vendors and pharmaceutical companies take inventory of where we all are today and draw a vision of where we are going.

## Also tell stories to yourself

In his book *Moonwalking with Einstein*, Joshua Foer tells a rollicking story about his journey behind the scenes of the world of memory championship; it's a great story about memory and storytelling. Among several memory building techniques he learns from the memory masters is a form of storytelling-based mnemonic premised on one of the great truths of what makes stories, and the people who tell them, memorable: humor.

Yes, humor.

The device requires that you first construct a mental palace with many rooms and then that for each room, you tell a little story to yourself about someone doing something in that room. The stranger the choice of person and of what he or she is doing, and therefore the more amusing, the better. Foer imagined the Incredible Hulk riding a stationary bike in his memory palace's front entryway, wearing large loopy earrings, Jerry Seinfeld sprawled out and bleeding on the hood of Lamborghini in the upstairs hallway, and Einstein moonwalking in one of the bedrooms. To memorize something complex —- such as the sequence of a whole deck of playing cards read out to him – he would associate three cards each with one of these strangely populated rooms, starting with the Hulk in the front entryway. So effective was this practice that Foer won the championship.

Remember him when you think up your stories.

You see, funny stories that are good are remembered better than just good stories.

The joy of a good joke was bred into us through evolution, and it seems to be shared around the animal kingdom. Hyenas may not really be laughing, but many types of primate have been observed to pull pranks on one another. In fact, as reported by *Slate*, one particularly astute gorilla has been observed to be real jokster.

> Nonhuman primates don't just laugh—there's evidence they can crack their own jokes. Koko, a gorilla in Woodside, Calif., who has learned more than 2,000 words and 1,000 American Sign Language signs, has been known to play with different meanings of the same word. When she was asked, "What can you think of that's hard?" the gorilla signed, "rock" and "work." She also once tied her trainer's shoelaces together and signed, "chase."

The article also reports that human laughter is thought to have evolved from the panting sounds that primates make when they are playfully rough-housing with  one another, thought to be a signal that it's all just in good fun.

If humor was selected for in the rough and tumble of nature's tooth and claw competition, it must serve a good purpose. Indeed, science suggests that humor has many mental and physical benefits. Laughing increases blood circulation in the lungs and muscles, strengthens our immune systems, boosts our energy, diminishes pain, and reduces stress. It also helps us bond; it can turn an awkward social encounter into the start of a new friendship, or a group of tough-sell buy-siders at a conference into your biggest fans.

Humor is the awesome sauce of storytelling. But you've got to be careful not to slather it on too thick. A good joke is funny, and short, and then the story is the equivalent of a class recess, or seventh inning stretch.  Be careful not to make it more than an opening shot or interlude. And always remember, sometimes humor is anything but funny. Comedy comes in three flavors, truth, fiction, and sheer stupidity.  Making the truth funny is the most delicate operation; it's not as much about what's said, as how it's said.  Chris Rock can get away with saying "A black man failing black history... ain't that some sad shit..... cuz you *know*, fat people don't fail cooking!" Russell Peters can pull off saying "Just for the record my Arab friends, I don't do any Arab jokes in my act. It's not that I don't think you are funny. It's just .. I don't know, I don't wanna..... die?"

If they weren't masters of delivery, they'd be on the most wanted list of every ethnic and religious group around the world.

Fiction is less tricky, because the audience immediately figures out your story isn't real. As for sheer stupidity, it works well for comedians – people love it because they believe they will never do something so stupid themselves. It makes them feel smarter. But sheer stupidity doesn't work well at the office.

So here is my best advice for telling stories:

1. Always tell stories that are positive; don't criticize your neighbor or boss just to be funny.
2. Stories should be about people; always make sure you include good characters, or use yourself as one; this helps with neural coupling.
3. Tell stories that people can relate to, and that won't offend them. Even a really funny story concerning religion may not get any laughs at a religious convention.
4. Start with a hook. For example, above I started my story with "Can anyone tell me why 5:05 p.m. sucks?" This gets people's attention, and never forget how many people in any audience are likely to be texting if you don't grab their attention.
5. Or, as an alternative, try starting with "Guys I am going to tell you a story, it's a good one, but bare with me." This invites folks in and does great mental prepping; they'll be more on your side because you've indicated you'd like to make things fun for them.

Don't be shy; give it a try. The more memorable you are, the more influence you will have and the more disruptive you can be, without getting fired...

*While writing this chapter, I listened to*
*Hotel California by the Eagles*

# INGREDIENT 3:

## *Be a teacher, even when you don't know squat*

In my experience, there is no better way to force yourself to learn something new than to teach it. The nineteenth century French philosopher Joseph Joubert wrote, "to teach is to learn twice." You can read as much as you like, and you can throw yourself into learning by doing. But when you have to teach someone something, you quickly discover that you must anticipate every question your students might possibly ask. You do not want them to stump you. Before long, you find yourself in the dungeons of knowledge, learning things you would have never cared to know, but not only will that knowledge often eventually be highly valuable to you, as you pass it on to others, you will gain the status of a guru. You'll also be recognized as a catalyst of innovation, and you'll build relationships across departments and teams that help your organization break down silos and develop more efficient and effective communication and collaboration. The organization will win, those you teach will win, and you will win; it's a win-win-win.

I'm not referring to going out and getting an adjunct professorship at a college, or teaching at a high school extension program, though both might be great things to do. I'm talking about teaching inside your company. This is done all the time, of course, by managers as well as peer to peer, through all of the small moments of training, collaboration and mentorship that go on day to day. But that's not what I mean. I mean actually giving classes.

How can you just start doing that in an organization though? Don't you need the permission of HR? And how likely is it you're going to get that? Good point. HR can be counted on to put up the most resistance. But what I want you to know is that you do not need permission. Three times in my career I have designed and taught courses to my colleagues, of my own volition, and in two of those cases, HR eventually embraced the classes and made them part of their standard offerings. Yes, I became that train the trainer guy.

In one of those cases, the first class I offered developed into an entire curriculum, which helped boost not only my career but those of two instructors who took my place developing it once I'd moved on. In all of these cases, I was teaching about topics I was not an expert on.

Which is why I will advise you that all it takes to become a good teacher is being good at research, not being afraid to get up in front of a room (practice some public speaking), knowing how to create some slides (but remember, stay away from the stultifying 20 card pack Power Point, focus on telling stories), and controlling your perspiration.

## I lost my shirt teaching

I began my career as a programmer, and I was lucky – for some reason my brain knew how to create code that not only worked but that got noticed. I loved the challenge and inventiveness of coding, and I would try all kinds of crazy things, typing away like a wild man. Sometimes other developers would stand behind me and watch me code. So I became known as a killer programmer, even after an unfortunate incident in which I brought down three CICS Regions by trying to write recursion in COBOL (don't worry, you don't need — or want — to know what that means; let's just say it's like trying to launch a bicycle into space by strapping a rocket engine on the back– it's a bad idea and things are going to break).

The programming we were doing when I was at Prudential Securities was all in COBOL, but Visual Basic was beginning to crowd COBOL out as the preferred language in the computing scene. I decided to teach myself VB, which I did by hacking chat rooms and newsgroups on AOL. (Back then hacking meant to learn something very fast by finding information others can't.) I was writing code in order to hack in and find information about how to write more and better code. Novel, at the time. A rumor once spread that I had broken into the Prodigy network (this was before America Online) with the home made broad band I had installed in my home basement — four 14.4K modems wired into borrowed phone lines (a trifle now, but a tower of connectivity then). In truth I had broken in just through some dexterous coding, it wasn't the modems.

I learned VB, but I was no pro. Still, I was way ahead of my programming colleagues, and as they began to fear losing their jobs to VB programmers, they started asking me to teach them.

After a while, enough had come to me that I decided to teach a formal class. What the hell? What did they know about VB? How likely was it that they would ask a question I couldn't answer? Still, when it came time for my first class, I was outrageously nervous. Fourteen people had signed up, and I had never met any of them. I had expected my students would all be people I knew, who worked in my group or on the same floor, and I knew they would cut me some slack. But here were fourteen total strangers; all eager to learn from the guy they'd heard was the killer programmer.

I perspired so much that first morning that my boss, who was sitting in the back of the room, suddenly got up and left. I thought my embarrassment was too much for her to take. But it turned out she went to the company store and bought me a shirt, which I changed into during the 10:15 to 10:30 break (true story).

Fast forward a bit, and I had trained over 1,500 COBOL developers on VB, and I then moved on to teaching C++, Java, JavaScript and early versions of XML, XSL and XSLT. I was still in my early twenties and I was known all around a Fortune 500 company as the guy who understood how to keep up with all of that mind-numbing tech stuff.

## The business they start may be your own

When I then moved to UBS Wealth Management, the CIO shared that she had a problem she couldn't figure out precisely how to solve. The developers lacked sufficient business knowledge to anticipate the bank's programming needs and to help the product team effectively in creating new products. The business side and the tech side just couldn't speak the same language. She had heard about my classes at Prudential Securities and wondered if I could create a teaching program for the development team. I developed a curriculum that I called "The Culture of Ownership," which taught programmers about the design of a large bank, the various divisions, what the divisions did, what types of customers large banks have, what products and services each customer segment potentially purchases, and how those products and services worked. I also reached out to other middle managers and asked them to design and teach classes, and soon we had created a mini-university. You cannot imagine the mileage I got from this.

The upper management loved the program and I was asked to give presentations about it at company town halls. I was also asked to develop metrics about how the program was driving significant performance gains and had vastly improved communication between the business and tech teams, leading to better products and more innovation. Ultimately, I was asked to present these findings to a number of executive steering committees as well as to our business partners, to demonstrate our corporate prowess.

After a couple of years, I passed on the leadership of The Culture of Ownership to someone else, but I continued to play a role in an advisory capacity, so I kept the glow of being the founder, but was freed up to move on to other projects. The guy who took over after me also got a career boost from leading the program, as did the guy who took charge after him, and I was able to find out that it even served as the basis for someone's startup.

## Don't eat Italian sausage and peppers in public

In the summer 2011, I was at a street fair in New York City and I didn't feel like counting calories. I was working my way through the crowd chomping on an Italian sausage and pepper sandwich in one hand, struggling with hot sauce leaking all over my face, hands and t-shirt, while also juggling a bottle of water and roasted corn-on-the-cob on a stick. I had made a bad purchasing decision.

Suddenly a woman ran up to me, extremely excited. She assumed I remembered her (I did vaguely, but had no idea what her name was) and she exclaimed to her husband, trailing right behind her with their children, "Honey this is the guy whose idea I stole!" I don't know who was more in shock, me or her husband, seeing his wife run up to this scrawny, unshaven Guyanese kid in a t-shirt and ripped jeans with what seemed like horrible eating habits.

It turned out that she had been laid off from the firm a few months back and she had decided to start a business based on the curriculum of The Culture of Ownership. I ended up hanging out with the family for two hours, shopping and playing games. Later I gave her some pro bono advice about how to update the classes. After all, she had started a business teaching what I initially taught here.

The time I spent teaching these classes was some of the most valuable in my career. I not only enjoyed the experience of witnessing the first receiver reach of teaching; I got a good deal of satisfaction from seeing the engagement of my colleagues in the classes and how we were all learning to work better together and innovate better. This was an additional payoff I never could have anticipated. I learned from this that teaching is like dropping a rock in water, it creates ripples of beneficiaries. Your students will teach others, and so on and so forth. And you never know the ways in which you may be empowering them.

## Helping people bake bread

Give someone a loaf of bread, and he will eat for a day, teach someone how to bake and she will eat for a lifetime. You'll also get fortifying sustenance for yourself. Teaching is the ultimate act of giving and giving is the most rewarding means of receiving. Teachers, mentors, and those my cousin Dhar told me about in India known as Gurukuls – who have students come and live with them – are the most fortunate of givers because there simply is no more valuable gift than knowledge.

I had no idea I'd ever teach people, and I had no training whatsoever in how to do it. You don't need it, because while there's no question that teaching is both an art and a science, we are all teachers. We teach every day; our friends and relatives, our children, people we meet at parties or conferences and want to know what we do. The office is inherently a classroom, but in too many it's only the managers who teach (or all too often fail to). Peer to peer teaching is vital. Studies of children's learning in education research have shown that kids learn more from teaching their peers than they do from being taught by their teachers, and leave it to the ancient Greeks to have understood its power. Aristotle appointed students as teachers way back in the first century AD.

Many people are afraid to teach because they don't think they know enough. I hope I've put the lie to that. But also consider this: work in brain science has shown that nothing is better for maintaining your memory and critical thinking skills as you age than continuous learning. And remember, there's no better way to learn than to teach. This is not to mention the threat of obsolescence. As the pace of technological change has quickened, the pace of change throughout all of work life has been cranked up, and those who don't constantly work out on the cognitive treadmill find themselves lapped by the new young things right out of college.

Finally, teaching your peers will grow your professional network, and the bonds you form will be especially strong. People establish more powerful and longer lasting ties when they share with each other to resolve problems. The alliances that emerge lead to all sorts of innovative ideas, and those results reinforce the bonds.

It's a virtuous cycle.

As the great American educator, historian and journalist Henry Adams wrote in his classic The Education of Henry Adams, "A teacher affects eternity; he can never tell where his influence stops."

*While writing this chapter, I listened to*
*American Pie by Don McLean*

# INGREDIENT 4:

## *Steal talent; do it publicly and build a reputation for it*

Okay, it must be said that before you start stealing talent – or at least at the same time — it's best to also cultivate your current talent. Unless you are building your own team from the ground up, which almost never happens in corporations, you are more than likely going to inherit the lion's share of your group. This can be frustrating because many of them may be people you wouldn't have chosen. This is why rule number one of management is: almost everyone can work for you (some few, there's no hope for). Rule number two is: For your people to work for you, you have to learn how to work for them first.

Anyone in an organization who honestly believes that you have his or her interest at heart can work well for you. One of the surest means of success is to put the success of others over yours. In leadership, the primary currency is influence, and there is no better way to exercise influence than to build allegiance. Linda Hill, the head of Harvard Business School's High Potential Leadership Program and of the Leadership Initiative stresses the importance of a new kind of leader for today's business world who shares power with his or her team, believes in the potential of ordinary people, and puts a good deal of emphasis on developing employees talents. Essentially, you want to purify your intentions publically, privately, and demonstrably enough that anyone who works for you will always answer when asked (and your people will be asked) that they trust you.

Now this is not to say that there aren't some people in whom it's hard to see the potential. I had one specific employee for two years who was extremely smart, who was humble but not meek. She never missed an opportunity to ask for more work, more responsibility, and to get involved. Initially I loved this, but all too soon I discovered that she would never finish anything. No matter what I tried, she would get the first 80% of a project done faster than anyone, but then never get to the last 20%. And, as I've learned over the years, the last 20% of anything is the most important 20%.

I didn't always have the perspective to see through people's weak spots like this. Then I watched the movie *The Great Gatsby*, which opens with the lines, spoken by the narrator Nick Carroway, "In my younger and more vulnerable years my father gave me some advice that I've been turning over in my mind ever since: Always try to see the best in everyone." The wisdom of that advice hit me hard. I realized that I'd benefited enormously from someone having done just that with me; he was the one who also taught me about stealing people.

Early on in my time at Lehman, one of the managing directors – a formidable guy who had been a managing director at Goldman Sachs earlier – called me into his office. I didn't report to him and I had no idea what he wanted with me. He stunned me by saying "I want to see you succeed. I know you have an unusual skill of being able to draw ideas." He chaired the steering committee for the Wealth Management Reporting project at Lehman, and he'd witnessed many of my presentations to the committee in which I used visuals to convey complex information simply. I spent a good amount of my time in the next two years at Lehman making drawings for him, even though I never worked for him. He had stolen me.

I created illustrations to convey the status of projects, to take the place of mind-numbing spreadsheets. I would find ways to illustrate the various features of some software in development which couldn't yet be demonstrated so that they could debate ways to go with it. I would craft drawings to depict when certain milestones would be reached to take the place of turgid status reports.

He had recognized a talent of mine and had looked past my "issues" as somewhat of a loose cannon. The work I did for him accelerated my career. Though at the start, he presented the illustrations I made for him, over time I was invited to present them myself and I was invited to more and more senior meetings. I got exposure to higher level discussions than I would not have had access to otherwise, I grew my network, and I got lots of practice presenting to large, senior, and many times difficult audiences! You can say I learned how to hold my own in front of a room all because of him.

Once I'd had my realization about seeing the best in my people as he had in me, I learned how to find the one unique thing about anyone and everyone who worked for me that I could help them make the most of. Research by Gallup suggest the basis of the popular Strengths Finder book and training program has shown that it's not by trying to train people into strengths that you get the best results, but by tailoring work for them that draws on the strengths they *do* have. That's absolutely worked for me.

But I also learned to start stealing people. And the thing about stealing people is that they are usually so relieved and happy to be tapped for their talent that they work harder for you than anyone else does. Over time, people who haven't reported to me have delivered even more for me than those actually under me on the organizational chart.

## How an intern became a white falcon

After I left Lehman I moved to a position as a director at UBS and managed a team of business analysts, developers and testers supporting the company's technology for "managed products," which included mutual funds, alternative investments such as hedge funds, and some financial planning and wealth planning tools. It was a cool job, the firm was pivoting to managed products, and we were in the middle of a massive transformation. I realized that the Natural User Interface was the future of financial planning tools and that we needed to upgrade our offerings, in particular by building touch screen applications. So I finagled the funding to purchase two Microsoft Surface tables – which were like coffee tables with touch sensitive screens installed — against the will of our CIO and CTO. (Awesome sauce, when poured on properly, can get things funded that no one agrees with.) Now I needed someone to do the coding on these touch enabled "coffee tables".

I wasn't close enough to coding anymore to do it myself, and no one on my team was up for the challenge; I had inherited some of the most risk averse folks I've met to date. So, I stole Chris Dutra. He was an intern, still in college, at the bank for his second tour, whom I had infected the year earlier, giving him lots of assignments. Now, coincidentally, he sat right in front of my new office. He wasn't reporting to me, but I discovered that he knew how to do the programming I needed. So I stole him.

I offered him the chance to write UBS's very first touch application. To smooth things over with the director he was actually reporting to, I suggested that the pilot be an application that director owned. So, in effect, I not only stole Chris, I stole his director. Eventually I stole his entire team. Turned out the programming was no easy feat, so many hands were needed.

The prototype application the team wrote garnered attention not only in the New York office, but from many regional CEOs as well as the global CEO, and Chris and the team were called on to demonstrate it to them. Many times with these demonstrations, I was not in the room. It's important when stealing people that you not also steal their credit. Making them look good makes you look good; trust me. Always, always give credit where credit is due. This is one of the best ways of putting others' success ahead of your concerns for your own, and the trust you will earn will repay you many times over.

It turned out that the corporate chiefs liked what they saw so much that the creation of that prototype spawned a touch and mobile innovation contest at the firm. It was a 90 day long contest of all developers in North America to write a touch application for the bank. Each team had an executive sponsor, and the prototypes were judges in a series of elimination rounds. For the announcement of the winner, over 250 people came from all around the company, operations, legal, the field, and human resources, to see the finalist applications. Chris headed up his team, and they became known as the White Falcons (I was the team's executive mentor).

This initiative launched UBS into mobile ahead of everyone else on Wall Street.

Before long, I was barely involved with anything concerning touch and mobile at the firm, because I moved on to other things, including social media and big data. Chris established himself as a stand-out – he wasn't just another Falcon, he was called "the Falcon," – and went on to spearhead some glorious projects. That, got him promoted out of programming, and eventually he left the firm to go change the world joining MicroStrategy, one of the leading providers of enterprise software.

What did I get out of it all? Well, for one thing, the CIO's global innovation award. But, of course, much more. By launching UBS out ahead of the Street in mobile, I built my reputation industry wide. More importantly, though, I got the enormous satisfaction of helping Chris catapult to success and find his calling, all while helping myself.

All I had to do was steal him.

## My own Alexander the Great

By 2011, I was being asked to speak at Wall Street conferences a great deal. I still marvel at how many folks asked me to speak on topics that I was not an expert on; often I was talking about things that weren't even any part of my day-to-day job. Lesson: the better public speaker you learn to be, the more people will think you know. This got to be truly bizarre; often I was sure that I knew the least in the room, yet there I was up on the podium. The more topics I was asked to speak about, the more presentation materials I needed. Eventually, I needed help putting them together.

So I stole Alex.

He worked for the guy in the office next to me. Rumor had it that Alex could make great digital drawings, and that he had an insanely quick brain. So, when one day I noticed Alex lingering near my office door – word had spread that if you hung around my office enough, I was likely to grab you and ask you to do some cool thing — I pulled him in. We chatted a bit and he confided in me that he was afraid he would get bored quickly in corporate life. I had just the thing to make sure his days were void of suck-dom.

Unlike Chris's manager, Alex's boss was not supportive of me stealing him, but I did it anyway, shamelessly and habitually. He was so good that he could deliver for his boss and have the time to also work for me. He drew everything for my presentations, creating awesome slides. I would just discuss my speech with Alex and he'd come back with the perfect images. He dove into the content and learned all about the horizons. Eventually I invited him to join me at conferences and I introduced him to many of my contacts. He even picked up many of my mannerisms; he became a mini-Richie, all in less than six months. I called him Alex the Great.

Then I left UBS, and most of my work with senior executives — researching new paradigms and the coming trends and assembling pitches to the technology investment governance steering committee — went to Alex. He was just 22! I benefitted from knowing someone brilliant was taking over for me, he benefitted by getting a big promotion within a year at the firm, and the firm benefitted because he was brilliant. The only one who maybe didn't benefit was his boss, who probably lost some sleep trying to figure out why Alex did so much work for me.

Talent is everywhere throughout any organization, and most of it is sorely underutilized. A recent Gallop survey found that around the world, only thirteen percent of employees are avidly engaged in their jobs. You may not think this is an issue you need to worry about. Surely you've got top talent coming to you and top talent is engaged. Well, research also shows that top talent really needs to be engaged and walks much faster. Case in point: Alex walked away from UBS only three months after I left. He'd been promoted into a great job, but it wasn't the same without the constant excitement of the challenges I'd thrown him.

 The sad truth is that few managers are good at motivating their talent. On the positive side, this is why there are always good people to steal.

Recognizing, borrowing, leveraging, and outright stealing talent displays a leader's resourcefulness and ability to draw talent in and allocate it for growth. There's a corrosive myth that great corporate leaders are the ones with the vision and the power — whether through exuding charisma or by cracking the whip – and that they make all the difference in a company's success. The truth is that the most successful leaders are those who know how to empower their people and allow them to voice *their* visions. The more I think about this, the more I become convinced that empowering people is *the* essential component of leadership.

Key to truly empowering people is giving them credit; this is the surest route to building trust. And research shows that employees' trust of their manager is a vital component of engagement, while the lack of trust is one of the biggest contributors to disengagement. By recognizing and recruiting talent to work for you, you display your genuine interest in helping others succeed. It is a sign of respect, and it builds trust.

The literature on leadership identifies four primary leadership styles: charismatic, servant, authentic, and transformational. A charismatic leader focuses on inspiration, charm, excellent communication skills, showing confidence in his or her abilities, and role modeling moral conviction, energy and enthusiasm. Transformational leadership emphasizes the articulation of a company vision and sets a mandate for innovation, inspiring and motivating people to think outside the box. Servant leaders put strong emphasis on the needs of others, above their own, and on sharing power, rather than wielding it. Authentic leadership is characterized by transparency, by a leader's recognition of his or her own strengths and weaknesses, and by consistency between what one says and what one does. To be a truly great leader, you must combine all four.

But I think the most fundamental truth of leadership is that to be an effective leader, you need followers. And the best way to attract followers is the selfless commitment to putting their careers in front of yours. You will not be truly successful until you help others succeed.

Steal those people and make them succeed, they will follow you in exchange.

*While writing this chapter, I listened to*
*Iris by the Goo Goo Dolls*

# INGREDIENT 5:

## *Be brutally honest, even when it hurts*

I follow sports closely because it's full of many inspirational success stories. It is the ultimate showcase of human determination, belief, and resilience. As I sat to write this chapter, I was watching an NFL special about legendary coach Bill Parcels, "A Football Life." As one would imagine, it was worth every minute of my time. The show chronicled the coach's rise from his humble beginnings to his induction to the Hall of Fame, with excerpts from an interview with him laced throughout. Near the end, the interviewer asked Parcels what the one thing that stood out and mattered the most in his career to him was. With glistening eyes, Parcells replied:

> "Early on my father recognized my love for football and pulled me aside one day and said, Bill, quit fooling around, God put you on this earth to be a football coach, your greatness lies ahead of you, but promise me one thing. When this football journey comes to an end, you will see an old man in the glass, and your happiness and success will be defined by how proud the old man will be of you. Be honest in whatever you do, because while you may fool others, you will never be able to fool the old man in the glass. You must to be prepared to live with what he sees."

Everybody's heard the old phrase "honesty is the best policy," but everybody also knows that practicing honesty isn't so simple. It's generally either too hard or too easy. Some people find it painfully awkward to share uncomfortable truths and fear the consequences; others will spit out the most offensive criticisms without compunction. Being honest with some people is easier than with others. Being honest about what is bad is much easier than being honest about what is good, and being honest with yourself is much more difficult than being honest with others. This doesn't mean it's not the best policy; it means that being honest takes some practice.

In my twenties I struggled quite a bit with being honest with bosses, colleagues and employees – as well as with everybody else in my life. I had been brought up to strictly follow the other old adage about honesty, "if you don't have something nice to say don't say anything at all". Then, a few years of into the pressure-cooker of Wall Street banking life, I became all too inclined to point out the bad, while being reluctant to call out the good, even when it was awesome.

Eventually I learned that failing to tell the truth – both good and bad – has a boomerang effect. You can get away with it for a while, but eventually it comes back to hit you smack in the face.

*Bob Marley — 'You can fool some people some times but you can't fool all the people all the time'*

One of the things that makes truth-telling so difficult is that while most of us claim to want to hear the truth, when presented with it, we so often go into denial. Our capacity to resist information that runs counter to our hopes and desires, or our cherished beliefs, or that undermines our sense of self, is astonishing. The field of decision science has identified a host of biases in our thinking, "wired" into our brains through the millennia of evolution, that subvert our ability to hear and see the truth. One is known as the self-serving bias, which causes us to take responsibility for successes while downplaying our role in failures. Another is the confirmation bias, which leads us to reject information or characterizations that don't confirm our deeply held views, whether about politics, God, a referee's call against our favorite team, or about ourselves. This bias can be so strong that it leads to the "backfire effect," when people dig in and become even stronger in their beliefs if confronted with contrary evidence.

Our brains seem to be stubbornly resistant to "replacement knowledge," not wanting to give the heave to accepted wisdom to make room for the new. If we're presented with information in the style of it being a contradiction, therefore, we often reject it. Which means that if we want people to see a truth they're denying, we've got to be clever. If replacement knowledge is presented as new knowledge without directly challenging the existing knowledge (or misconception) then it's much more often accepted. It's a form of magic.

*It's like a good card trick, you are not sure how your mind was manipulated.*

So while I'm saying to be brutally honest, I don't mean to be blunt. Being a good truth teller takes some finesse. It also takes learning to be more self-aware; to be honest with yourself. You have to learn to think about your thinking, and to audit your actions. What we really think and what we say are very often quite different, as are what we do and what we think we do, and what we think versus what's the truth. The first requirement of being honest with others is to get much better at being honest with ourselves, and that means being willing to be self-critical, not only with ourselves but with others.

You have to become an auditor of your own thinking and behavior. This will not only keep you from digging in when you should make a pivot; it builds trust that is invaluable. And the more honest you are about your own failings, the more people will like and respect you.

## It took me a year to understand unitization

I was once in charge of a transformation project at Lehman Brothers in which one of the major goals, I was told, was to "unitize hedge fund partnership accounting." Apparently, this would allow for reporting on hedge fund earnings in the same way as earnings from any other investment instruments, such as mutual funds and individual equity stocks. "Unitization" was the buzzword; everyone knew what it meant. And because I was young and seemed to be plugged in, everyone on the transformation teams assumed that I knew what it meant as well. The truth is I didn't, and I struggled leading the teams because I lacked the fundamental knowledge of just what it was we were trying to accomplish. But I didn't tell anyone.

Finally, about a year into the project, I stopped a steering committee meeting and said "Hey guys, this is embarrassing, but I really don't understand unitization completely and I would like to be taught about it from the ground up". After some laughter, we discussed the topic for an hour, and we discovered that many in the room didn't understand unitization. I came to be seen as the courageous honest guy (even though it had taken me a year to divulge the truth).

The result was that we put the multi-year project on hold and held what we termed "requirement immersion sessions" for two weeks. About twenty or thirty project members spent the entire day each day for those two weeks going line-by-line, page-by-page through the project requirements and making sure everyone understood every difficult topic. Guess which subject took the lion's share of the day almost every day? Yep, unitization.

One day before I left the firm, I happened to hear something really cool. A very senior manager said on a conference call "guys I'm having a unitization moment, I don't understand..." I was floored. It seemed there was a new willingness among at least some around the company to be honest about what they didn't know.

## Be honest, but don't carry a big stick

While I was working at UBS complaints were flooding in from financial advisors — ultimately 7,000 of them — saying that the software the bank had provided them, written by the bank's IT staff, was difficult to use. The leadership team rallied, seizing the opportunity to create another committee — the User Experience Committee, or what I later termed the worst way to waste two hours of twenty-plus individuals' time every two weeks. I questioned the composition of the committee, because it consisted largely of managers and leaders who had been involved in building the sucky software currently being complained about, and it didn't include enough of the users or representatives of the users. I knew we were in trouble when instead of diving into what was working with the software and making improvements from there, we began by setting forth a set of design guidelines, prioritizing the applications by suck-dom according to the guidelines, and then decided to tackle the worst ones first. We paid no attention to what worked and why it worked, only what was broken. Ass backwards.

The meetings became so tedious that I simply stopped going. I had realized by then that one of the best ways to get time back in my day was to not attend the meetings that wasted my time. I got a lot of smack for it, but most of those on the committee I talked to about it told me they would have loved to do the same thing but didn't dare (fear of being fired).

I got called back in about three months later, told in no uncertain terms to attend the next meeting, because I was leading the development of an application that was violating all of the design rules set forth by the committee. So I went, and boy did I go. I prepared a dossier of every member of the committee, his or her experience, and the applications each had been in charge of developing. I had also interviewed some users about their (poor) experiences with the applications, and I laid bare those faults. I even redesigned a few of the applications owned by committee members with the design principles I had applied in the new "renegade" app. I made one hell of a slide presentation at the meeting.

Shortly after that, the financial market melted down and the committee was forsaken. The bank churned through two CEOs in two years, and everything was completely different and new. I don't know what would have happened if all hell hadn't broken loose as I told the truth in the meeting. The ugly truth, that the committee could not be responsible for setting design principles, because no one on the committee understood design! Maybe I would have found I'd tried a little too hard to be fired. As things came to pass, though, I was appointed to be chair of yet another committee, the Customer Experience Committee, to institute a more user-friendly approach to software product development and I was called into just about every design session about every new app to think through the user experience. (So I guess I got what was coming to me, more work.)

In hindsight I can see that I was being the proverbial bull in a china shop calling them all out that day, and I've learned in the years since that while it is important to be brutally honest, it's also important to do it without arrogance. Your awesome sauce should be piquant, but you don't want it to leave a bad taste in the mouth.

Honesty, even though I was arrogant that time, got me in the driver's seat of setting design principles for UBS application portfolio.

*While writing this chapter, I listened to*
*Since U Been Gone by Kelly Clarkson*

# INGREDIENT 6:

## *Draw everything, resist the urge to write*

E arlier I argued that a story is worth a thousand pictures. Well, that was a bit of hyperbole to stress the value of stories. Now I'm going to make the case for pictures.

The origin of the well-known adage "a picture is worth a thousand words" is murky. Some claim it's a derivation of a phrase coined by the ancient Chinese philosopher Confucius, and that the original posited that a picture equates to *ten* thousand words. Others claim the phrase originated in ancient Japan. The modern popularization of the phrase is easier to pin down. The esteemed newspaper editor and editorialist Aurthur Brisbane gave a speech in 1911 to the Syracuse Advertising Men's Club in which he advised "Use a picture. It's worth a thousand words." The phrase was quoted in an article covering the speech and it took off from there. Before that, many ads were packed with prose and featured no images. Take a look at this one for cigarettes from the late 1880s:

Compare that to the original ad featuring the Marlboro Man:

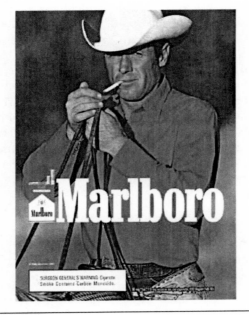

Just one word. (Well, except for the Surgeon General's Warning, which, of course, no one paid any attention to at all.) *Advertising Age* magazine named it the number one ad of the twentieth century.

We all understand how powerful images can be; paying close attention to images is as deeply imbedded in our nature as is fear. The drawing of pictures predated the invention of writing, and there can be no doubt about how talented some early artists were. The paintings in the caves of Lascaux in France depicting horses, lions, and bears, as well as several extinct species such as mammoths, aurouchs and ibices, are said to be so superbly crafted that in the low glow of flickering fire light, as the early humans huddled in the caves, the images would have seemed to move — perhaps the earliest form of animation.

Okay, so why, then, do so many people put slides like this one up at presentations?

Definitely one of the meetings that would allow me to get some time back in my day by not attending it.

Of course, one reason we don't use images more in our day-to-day business is that we think we don't know how to draw. I want to disabuse you of that notion. So, let me ask you, do you think you could learn to do this:

How to draw a stick figure

Those are the instructions of Dan Roam, author of *Back of the Napkin*, a fantastic book about drawing as a solution tool in business.

Or how about this, this is a recent mock up of the image I made in PPT in a few minutes, the real image used is a few pages in.

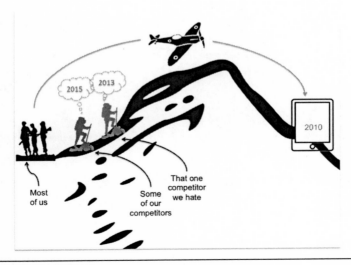

That image managed to finally convince the CEO of one of the companies I worked for in the early 2000s (which shall remain nameless so as not to embarrass anyone at the firm) that the company should become an early mover into the mobile tech space.

## The war for mobility

A number of us at the firm had been exploring the value of moving into providing mobile products, and we'd done a good deal of research and come up with what we thought was a very compelling case for making a ten million investment in purchasing mobile devices, bringing in talent, building the infrastructure and doing the continuing research to offer our clients top-quality mobile services ahead of the pack of our competitors. But the investment governance committee, which had to approve all such significant investments, had refused to approve the funding. We had gone back with an even stronger case, and still the committee turned us down. It was bizarre. We had broken the process down into easily managed phases, we had found vendors willing to partner with us to "de-risk" the investment, and we had even lined up early adopter users who had agreed to sponsor the investment, which had allowed us to generate a well-founded p&l clearly demonstrating that the move would drive above the line revenue.

How could they possibly be so ignorant?

I concluded that our CEO simply did not understand what we were saying. So in cahoots with one of my mentors at the firm, who was on the investment governance committee, I drew the simple image on the next page. It was simple, but it was based on some research. I had determined where each of our top nine competitors were moving into mobile products and found that some were lagging, like us, but others were somewhat on the way, and a few were further along. We'd be way behind before long if we didn't get going.

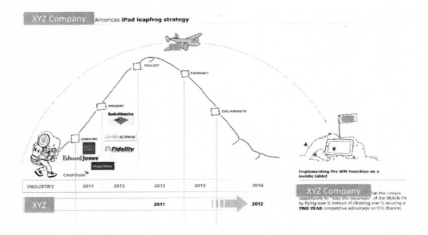

Just how the mobile space was going to develop was still fairly unclear, but two things were perfectly clear: there would be an intense competition, a real battle; and it was going to take a lot of learning to get there. So I drew a battlefield, with a large mountain in the middle of it, with all of us competitors fighting and climbing away on one side, and some starting to find some footholds, struggling to be the first to get to the other side and claim the riches of the lush new land of mobility.

The final flourish was the airplane soaring up over the mountain; my representation of how our firm could bound (leapfrog) right over the battle. My mentor loved the drawing and he showed it to the CEO in a casual conversation in the hallway. The project was funded in about three weeks – out of the cycle of the committee meetings — and I was told (though I'm not sure this is true) that the CEO pinned the drawing up in his office and left it there for months, referring to it in many of his discussions about the initiative.

## How to make even black holes and protein folding immediately comprehensible

I don't know if you've ever read about the physics of black holes, but aside from some cool factoids about how if you were to fall into one you'd be stretched out like a string of spaghetti – a process the astrophysicist Sir Martin Rees dubbed "spaghettification" – and how the smallest thing in the universe is the "singularity" at the center of a black hole, trying to understand them can be a real slog. What, for example, is a singularity? Or consider this breezy explanation of them from Wikipedia:

> The theory of general relativity predicts that a sufficiently compact mass will deform spacetime to form a black hole. Around a black hole, there is a mathematically defined surface called an event horizon [YOU CAN STOP READING NOW; POINT MADE. AN EVENT HORI-ZON??] that marks the point of no return. The hole is called "black" because it absorbs all the light that hits the horizon, reflecting nothing, just like a perfect black body in thermodynamics. [Quantum field theory in curved spacetime predicts that event horizons emit radiation like a black body with a finite temperature. This temperature is inversely proportional to the mass of the black hole, making it difficult to observe this radiation for black holes of stellar mass or greater.

Now look at this:

Which way would you rather learn about them?

One of the most mindboggling things in all of science is the mathematics of protein folding; proteins are unbelievably complex little structures. I could prattle on and on about that, but I would never, ever be able to convey that they look like this:

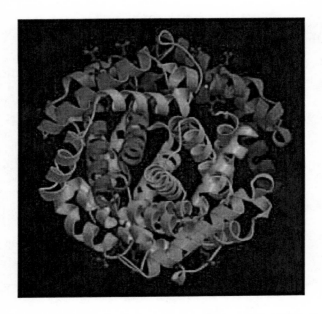

Of course these are examples of enormously sophisticated graphic artistry. And we all know images are tons of fun when it comes to science. But even the simplest, most amateurish drawings can be hugely effective, and they work wonders in the business world too.

On the occasion of Thomas Edison's 166th birthday General Electric offered people the opportunity to go onto Twitter, at #IWantToInvent, and use a drawing program to make blueprints of inventions they dreamed up. They came up with some fantastic ideas:

My secret is that I draw in PowerPoint, yes PowerPoint you heard it right. No need for sophisticated drawing software. Here are the things you need to know.

1. Cropping – In PowerPoint you have to get comfortable with cropping and resizing images.
2. Transparency – any object that is painted in PPT can have a transparency to it, this gives you depth in your drawings.
3. Removing Backgrounds – you can take just about any image from the Internet and make the background transparent! This is huge.
4. Layers – the order in which things are placed over each other can be a powerful drawing tool.
5. Cartooning – you can draw on a piece of paper, or white paper, take pictures of it, then make said cartoon a part of your PPT. The trick is to crop it right, and make the white/paper background transparent.
6. Alignment – nothing makes a PPT slide look better than good alignment, this adds a level of professionalism and presents the visual in a way where the brain receives it without questioning it.
7. Spacing – equal and thoughtful spacing is important, these are all easy to do.

The fact that images are so effective as communication is, of course, blatantly obvious — the images speak for themselves about that. But there are a few somewhat less obvious points worth making about their power. For one, if you stick with describing an idea, concept or some procedure, say the Bessemer process (the method of removing the impurities of iron in making pure steel), you leave it to the imaginations of those in your audience to create an image of what you're describing. And a problem here is that they are likely to create a whole range of different images.

But you want them to see the correct image. By drawing it for them, you clarify and standardize the image people will take away with them. This helps with neural coupling, which we discussed during the stories chapter.

Also, if you do the visualizing work for them, their minds are freed up to focus more on what you're telling them. Say you're making an argument for killing a product line. Let's say the product is Twinkies. Well, Twinkies have been an (unhealthy) staple of the American diet for decades. They've got their fans, and in fact after the Hostess snack cake line was sold off when the company went bankrupt, the new owner brought Twinkies back to stores with the marketing slogan "The Sweetest Comeback in the History of Ever." So, there you are advising that your company discontinue this venerable delight. Most likely, some of the people you're making the case to will be involved in their production or marketing. While you're making your pitch, they're likely to be preoccupied with counterarguments. But what if you show them a picture of a slim and fit Twinkie? Have you seen the Skinny Girl cocktail brand? Skinny Twinkie?

Good visuals help us have 'ah ha" moments. I was reminded of this effect recently when I gave a speech at a big life sciences conference.

## My doctor is my first second opinion

I was asked to speak at the conference about the future of the pharmaceutical industry, which I've been doing research and consulting in of late. There were lots of issues I could have covered, such as the problem of patent cliffs (the drastic loss of revenue starting at many companies when their patents for superstar drugs expire soon) and the effects of the recent regulatory changes in healthcare, otherwise known as Obamacare. But those issues have all been covered extensively in the press.

As I thought about how I could discuss something more original, it dawned on me that while most life sciences companies were in the process of "pivoting to the patient" — going direct to patients with more of their marketing efforts because they're getting less and less access to healthcare providers (doctors) so have less opportunity to influence them to write one drug into a prescription over another — no one had really done a good job of articulating why the patient mattered so much. The need to be more patient-focused wasn't just a matter of lack of access to doctors, I realized, it was part of much more profound shift going on in medicine.

My research into the changing medical ecosystem had revealed that many patients these days are going into a doctor's office having already diagnosed themselves. And this self-diagnosis is not the stuff of mere hunches, as in the past — I suspect I have appendicitis, or my friend had the same thing and so I know I have it too. This is self-diagnosis that is extensively researched, derived from the use of online resources like WebMD.com, patient social networks, scholarly research journals and the medical journals, and the access provided by the FDA to information about drug efficacy and risks. We are in the era of "democratized diagnosis," and I concluded that the role of the doctor will be changing. Doctors will be called on by patients not as *the* source of expert diagnosis, but as the one to give a "second opinion," so to speak, on the patient's research.

I did some more research, discussing the phenomenon with some leading industry participants and analysts, and gathering data about the trends, such as the increasing number of hits on WebMD, and the rising volume of healthcare related conversations going on in social networks. As I talked with people, I found that while most listened attentively, they weren't convinced about my scenario; they still believed in the sanctity of the doctor's expertise and didn't think it would diminish. I realized from this that most executives in life sciences don't think about what patients do before and after a doctor's visit. So for the presentation at the conference, I decided I would draw them a picture to show them.

In the center I drew an image of a doctor in his office, as if in a bubble:

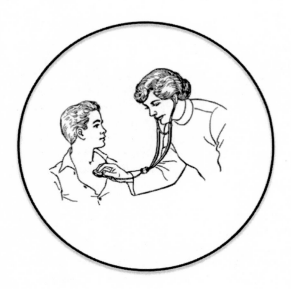

sanctity

Then, on the left, I drew an image of a patient three days before his doctor's appointment, getting all sorts of information about his ailment from multiple sources:

## democratization

And finally I drew an image the patient walking into the doctor's office thinking to himself, in a thought bubble, "I need the doctor to give me a second opinion," and then walking out of the doctor's office on his way to the pharmacist with another thought bubble saying "I am going to need a third opinion."

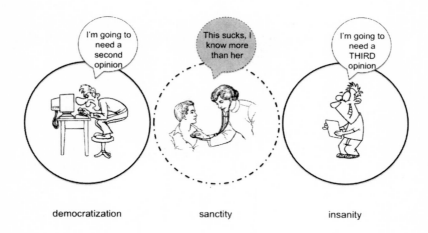

democratization       sanctity       insanity

I decided it would be the only image I would use in my speech. But I didn't put it up right away, I spoke about the drivers first, and the current schools of views on today's reality, and a few alternatives of what may or may not look like in the future. I told a story about a specific patient, and a specific doctor. Then I unfolded the image on the screen, and waited in 2-3 minutes of blissful silence.

I then covered all kinds of great subjects. I talked about the democratizing of the diagnosis process and how it is happening across cultures, across generations, and across disease classes. I discussed how health information is becoming a commodity, and the rate at the information readily available is exploding. I compared the changes under way to similar transformations occurring in the legal and financial industries, and I challenged the notion of the cruciality (the buzz word often used in the industry) of the doctor's expertise. I got a great response, with my Twitter and LinkedIn accounts flooded with comments. Some people even asked me if I wanted to start a business with them enabling a marketplace of opinions to be bought, traded and challenged between doctors and patients. The timing is still not right for that. But the best thing that happened was that a very well respected senior executive, with an important job at a very large firm, whom I had noted was sitting in the audience, walked up to me after the talk and asked "can I get a copy of that image?"

I could have used tons of charts full of reams of data to make my case, but I assure you no one would have asked me for those slides.

# I can't remember a word he said

Think about it. How many talks have you gone to that you would be able to summarize at all well even a week later? Now, think about how Steve Jobs used to make his new product introductions. I'll bet you can envision him perfectly, up there on that bare stage in his black turtleneck and jeans with a huge image of an iPhone behind him. His launch of the iPhone may have been the single most effective launch of a product ever; the glorious image of that gorgeous, ultra-cool object said it all.

Images leave a more lasting impression in our minds. Our minds are so attuned to them that we can even perceive them subliminally; we aren't consciously aware that we've seen them, but our mind has taken them in. Advertisers used to have all sorts of fun with that. You can check out those that CBS News dubbed the ten best ever made here: http://bit.ly/SubAds

As with stories, images appeal not only to our rational mind, but to our basic human needs; they ignite our emotions. Which explains why social media has gone so visual.

So learn how to draw. There's no excuse not to; the programs are a snap to use and PowerPoint can get you 80% of the way there. Or, if you're really determined it's not for you, then steal someone to do it for you!

Or, find freelancers on elance.com, taskrabbit.com or fiverr.com.

*While writing this chapter, I listened to*
*Ring of Fire by Johnny Cash*

# INGREDIENT 7:

## *Don't let your momma brand you; no one's buying it*

B ack in 2012, I was invited to speak on a panel at a reputable Wall Street women's event on the value of mobility in a financial services business model. Hard to believe, I know, that in 2012 that could still be a topic worthy of a panel discussion; the value of mobility should have been blazingly obvious by then. But I agreed to do it because I had left Wall Street about six months earlier and I thought it was a good time for a catch up.

There was a talk before the panel by a math geek (I mean management consultant) who talked for the fifty millionth time about how the mobile epidemic was coming. He paused for great emphasis when he imparted the killer slogan "tablets are not computers." (Fast forward two years and what do you know, tablets are computers.) The audience was comatose.

At least they got a little excitement watching those of us on the panel get up on stage and test our microphones. The moderator was an editor of a prominent magazine covering innovation, and the other panelists were two management consultants and two guys who worked in mobile technology for leading edge firms. The moderator's first question was "How do you make the case for mobility to executives?" I could see the room silently groan in disappointment. One of the management consultants snatched the question and babbled for a couple of minutes about some jazzy new acronym for a method for doing so, ending with the invaluable pearl of wisdom "you have to align business and technology." I cringed. The audience looked almost angry now, at least those who weren't typing on their Blackberries and smart phones.

About ten minutes in, the moderator addressed another of her scintillating questions to me. Deflecting, I said "Hey if it's ok, I'd like to go back to the first question and answer it. Two things. First, I started working on Wall Street twenty years ago, and on my first day I was given a pep talk about the need to align business and technology. If your company hasn't done that yet, you need to stop working there. Second, the foundation of financial services is the information supply chain. Mobile devices are democratizing the chain and transforming the relationship between a client and a banker. If you still have to describe this to your executives, and you can't explain to them that the glass that was once between the teller and the client, is now the glass on a mobile device, then you have bozos for executives and you should stop working there."

The audience came alive. Many heads were shaking up and down. A bunch of hands shot up with questions for me. And I know that many people in the room remembered my name, because I had twenty or thirty emails from people in the audience by the time I got home that night. The best thing, though, was that a young Asian woman who had just recently immigrated to the U.S. came up to me after the panel and asked "Can you mentor me? I would like to be able to tell what I know the way you do."

It's by speaking so forthrightly so often that I've become known as a provoker; that's become my brand. I know it's one of the main reasons I get invited to give so many speeches. I didn't choose the brand for myself, I was told I was a provoker by one of my mentors and I had to admit the label fit. Earlier in my career, my brand was that I was a sharer, which I adopted when, again, someone I worked with described me that way. My brand has changed because I've changed. I've become much more outspoken.

Lots of people misunderstand the notion of a personal brand. It's not a message you craft about yourself. Personal branding is like stand-up comedy. Anyone can get up on a stage at an open mic night and tell jokes, but you're not a comedian until the audience laughs at them. You don't have a personal brand because you tell people what it is; you have it because people tell *you* what it is. You can say what the heck you want about yourself, but that won't be your brand until someone else says it about you. So, the first thing to know about personal branding is that authenticity is vital.

Being brash wouldn't work for me if I didn't really have the compulsion to say it like I see it. Your brand isn't personal advertising. It is the truth about who you are and what you represent. It arises out of your vision, values, goals, skills, and passions. You should never have to fake your personality to impress others or feel pressured into changing who you are. Your disposition may not always be popular or politically correct, but if it's genuine, even your adversaries will respect you.

The second thing to know about personal branding is that we all have three brands (a) how our mom describes us, (b) how we describe ourselves and (c) how our co-workers and colleagues describe us. It's only brand (c) that anyone but you and your mom are going to believe about you.

The third thing to know about personal branding is that you want your brand to be convergent. I learned this from an angel investor I got to know. After three years of working with him, I asked him "how do you describe happiness?" I was floored by his answer. He said, happiness is when your personality in the conference room matches that of your personality in the living room. I have been striving to attain that ever since. Before that I thought of my work life and my personal life as independent of each other. Lots of people will object, but I am now totally convinced that my angel investor friend is absolutely right. The more you are the same person at work as you are in your personal life, not only the happier you'll be, but the more powerful your personal brand will be. This convergence may take some work. I've learned to allow some of the gentle lamb my mom thinks I am (I do have at least a little of that in me) to soften the hot-head I was at work when I was younger, and I've ended up as a provocateur.

## Find out about your brand messaging

What's your brand? How do you know? Pay attention to what those you work with say about you. If your boss tells you one day you're a catalyzer, think about how you've been catalyzing and lean into it. Maybe someone in sales tells you you're a rainmaker; definitely lean into that. I know someone who was once told in an annual review that he was the home run hitter on his team. Find out what people say about you. Go ahead and ask people how they see you (probably only those who know you pretty well.) Don't try to label yourself. Let other people do your brand messaging.

When I was hired as a Group Vice President at Cegedim, I asked my boss to describe my job in one sentence. She said "make the company cool again." I knew that was going to take plenty of provoking. Six months in, I asked some colleagues on the Executive Committee to describe me, and one of them said "chief glass breaker." I loved it. Most times transformational change management means you have to break things. About one year in, I asked one of our top sales representatives to describe me, and she said "chief infector." I'd progressed from breaking things to spreading my vision. Perfect. Lately I asked my boss to describe my role again and she said "the guy who brings out the best in others." That's the best branding I've had yet!

Don't focus on crafting a brand for yourself, just be authentic, and good at what you do. An authentic, strong personal brand builds trust and aligns expectations with what you have to offer. When people trust in what you've got to give, that trust leads to a more positive perception of your value. You are more distinctive; you become the go-to person for what you do.

Oh, and while you may not be the cherub your mother thinks you are, she doesn't have to know that. Mothers should be an exception to the convergence rule.

*While writing this chapter, I listened to
Careless Whisper by George Michael*

# INGREDIENT 8:

## *Make meetings shorter, and walk out on long ones*

One of the most precious raw materials in the world is time. When you waste time, no matter how smart you are, or how well you can execute, or what your title is, people will not see you as awesome. Wasting time is the opposite of awesome sauce; it tells people that you are just regular, unbranded, generic sauce.

Got it? Then, if you want, skip ahead to the next chapter.

See what I did there? I'm letting you take back some time. That's one of the most piquant ingredients of awesome sauce. Trust me, people absolutely love it. Even if they don't appreciate right away that they love it, they will eventually, like that satisfying feeling on your tongue after a good dash of hot sauce has lost its sting.

### Walking out on a steering committee at Lehman

I was under thirty and was an Assistant Vice President (which means nothing) at Lehman, and I was on the steering committee, which held a weekly two-hour meeting. One week, the agenda was to discuss whether a bug that had been found in a piece of software during quality assurance testing was a severity one (sev1) or a severity two (sev2) problem. (Sure you don't want to skip ahead to the next chapter?) The challenge was that if it was a sev1, it had to be fixed, which would delay the project about one week. If it was a sev2, it could be thrown over to the next release of the software. We'd then keep the project on schedule and deliver the software on time. Taking part in this debate were two managing directors, four senior vice presidents, two vice presidents, myself, and some software developers and testers.

Almost a dozen knowledge workers, including two high level executives, debating for what was scheduled to be two hours whether a year-long project should be delayed by one week or not. Let me do the math; at issue was a 1.9% extension of the timeline, and the bug was not material, meaning it posed no danger of incorrect reporting, no compliance risks, and no risk to revenues. I was the lowest level title in the room, and if you've ever worked on Wall Street, you know that means you are supposed to only speak when spoken to. But I couldn't take it. About half way through the meeting, I lost it.

I could not believe that this was why I had gone to college and was now getting my MBA; that this was why I had woken up nice and early, shaved (which I resent having to do), and put on a crisp shirt, a tie and a jacket. To sit there talking about this inane issue. I picked a moment and blurted out, "Hey guys, what do you think our hourly average salary rate is?" Some of them were clearly pissed at me, some just ignored me, some laughed, and others I could tell were eagerly anticipating the meeting melt down that was about to ensue. It got ugly. But I pressed on, and I got them to agree to 200 bucks an hour. Then I said, "Okay, so we are wasting 4,800 bucks of the firm's money trying to make this decision." (That was a low ball number; if I had added all the prep time that had gone into making the deck – yes, of course, we'd been shown a power point presentation about the "problem" — as well as the conversations that led up to the meeting (the meetings before the meeting), we had probably wasted more like $10,000 in our time alone, not to mention the opportunity costs of the actually money-making business we might have done with that time, which were probably much higher.)

I was determined to get fired that month, so I went one step further. I told them, "I am the least important here, right? And I am going to get up and leave and go do something meaningful with my time," and I walked out. I learned later that they all left after five more minutes and delegated the decision to the head of quality assurance and the program manager for the project, and that they had said they were okay with either decision, sev1 or sev2.

Now I'll let you in on a little secret about trying to get fired. On the days when you know you're close, do not leave the office before 10:00 p.m. You MUST wait. Eventually, someone higher up will come over to your office and talk to you. If you leave earlier, you really put yourself at risk. So I waited that day, and at about 7:15 p.m. my phone rang. It was the senior vice president I reported to, and he called me in to his office.

He was really upset about what I'd done and he told me to never do anything like that again. But he also told me that (1) the committee had decided to create a set of guidelines about what levels of decision had to be made by the committee (which would not include those about software bugs), (2) the meetings were now going to be one hour as the rule, with two hours as the exception, and (3) I was off the steering committee. Well, two out of three ain't bad.

I worked at Lehman for about two more years, and I can tell you this; several times the word came around in my division that a weekly meeting was going to be thirty minutes as the rule and one hour when needed, or one hour as the rule and two hours when needed. The culture had changed from one with a habit of long meetings as the rule and short ones as the exception, to short meetings as the rule and long ones as the exception. Also, at my going away party, every single one of the managing directors, senior vice presidents and vice presidents who were in the steering committee meeting the day I walked out came over to say goodbye. Every single one.

Always remember that people respect you when you help them not waste time.

## I ended a sales meeting 45 minutes early when I was the one doing the selling

Fast forward a few years and I'm working as Group Vice President of Digital Innovation at Cegedim. I am now in charge of many meetings, sales, projects, clients, innovation, press coverage, and some marketing, and I've made it my signature to keep all of them to 15 minutes, insisting on two things: proper introductions of all those attending at the start, and proper goals being set forth. When I absolutely have to hold a longer meeting, I keep it to 30 minutes and I always try to give people 5 minutes back. This is really, really important. You do not want people walking away from your meetings thinking; man did I waste time there.

Let me show you how well this works. One day, my team had an important sales appointment with a potential client. I took my account executive with me, my pre-sales engineer and one of our product experts. The meeting was scheduled for two hours, and it was a two-hour drive away. After we did a little get acquainted chit chatting, and our proper introductions, we dove into our presentation. About an hour into the two hour schedule, and half way through our fabulous slide deck, the client, who was the CIO of the company, got up and high-fived me. I knew then the meeting was over. I said to my team, "ok guys, this meeting is over, lets go home, the CIO just high-fived me."

Everyone chuckled. But I was serious. My account executive was hell bent on continuing with the slide deck, and it took me about 10 more minutes of diplomatic maneuvering to get him to stop. At which point I said to the CIO, "Hey, we are done here, you love us, we love you, let's let the next steps be figured out by the experts. Would you like to get 45 minutes back in your day?" He said, "Yeah but you guys drove two hours, I want to give you your full time." I told him we were good, and I got up and wrangled my team out of the room.

Out in the parking lot, they told me I had blown it, because we hadn't gotten to the pricing slide. But not only did we close the deal, the CIO and I became friends, and he still loves to tell the story about how I gave him back 45 minutes in his day. Now when I ask him for a favor, I always start with," Hey I need five of those 45 minutes back, can we talk?"

## We must use time as a tool

President John F. Kennedy, whose time in life was tragically cut short, gave a speech to the National Association of Manufacturers in which he said "We must use time as a tool, not as a couch." Think about that every time you plan a meeting. Is it going to be a couch for people to hang out on and take a break from the day, or a tool for really getting something done?

If you really have to hold a meeting, make it as short as you possibly can. The maximum attention span of adults involved in a task has been widely studied and estimates differ from just 10 minutes to about 45 minutes. Let's assume the best-case scenario; that gives you 45 minutes for holding an effective meeting, max. But I'd say that is only true if a meeting is well run and the person or persons running it are compelling. Let's face it, not everyone hosting meetings has any skill at it.

How often have you sat through a meeting that felt twice as long as it really was? This is a real phenomenon. Time can also seem to speed up. The perception of time is highly subjective. Research in cognitive science has shown that when we're deeply engaged in a task, we can get into the mental state known as "flow," when we utterly lose track of time. Three or four hours can go by in what feels like ten minutes. I love the story of a study done by French geologist and cave explorer Michel Siffre back in the early 1960s, at the height of the Cold War space race.

No one knew what might happen to people confined for long periods traveling in space, and one big question was how they would be affected by not being exposed to the regular cycle of the sun rising and setting – for astronauts orbiting in space, there are no sunrises; the sun just looks like another star, but a whole lot bigger. Here's a shot of it taken from the International Space Station, courtesy of NASA.

Siffre decided to live in a cave, 375 feet underground, with no means of telling time for two months. When he got the word from those monitoring him to come out, the date was September 14 but he thought it was August 20th. Above ground when he tried to measure out two minutes by counting up to 120 at one-second intervals, it took him 5 minutes. After emerging from the cave he estimated the trip had lasted 34 days. He'd actually been down in the cave for 59 days. His experience of time was rapidly changing. From an outside observer's perspective he was slowing down, but the psychological experience for Siffre was that for him, time was speeding up.

The opposite happens in meeting rooms. We become hyper–aware of time passing, and 45 minutes feels like 90 minutes. This is probably the key reason why those who are handcuffed to sit through boring meetings feel they've been a waste of time. You may well have an agenda worth 45 minutes, but if it feels like it's taken 90 minutes, people are going to feel it's been a time suck.

Just pause for a (brief) moment and consider this: time can seem to pass more quickly when you're all alone in a dark cave 375 feet underground than it does in many business meetings.

## Time really is money

The other reason long meetings are to be avoided at all cost is … their cost. Benjamin Franklin famously said, "Time is money," and he wasn't just being clever. We think of Franklin these days primarily as a Founding Father and flyer of kites into thunderclouds, but he was a highly successful entrepreneur fascinated by innovation. He started his own newspaper and he devised many ingenious inventions, such as bifocal glasses, swimming fins and, appropriately even the odometer — for the purpose of making postal delivery more efficient — as well as daylight savings time.

When he said time is money, he knew of what he spoke.

Some economists have actually devised means of calculating the cost of time wasted in business meetings. I don't know how this number was calculated, so I certainly can't say it's definitive, but one estimate is that it amounts to a whopping $37 billion in the U.S. annually. No wonder, really, when you consider that research shows that we hold an estimated 11 million business meetings a year, and that approximately half of that time is wasted. And this isn't just an American problem. Another study estimated that the annual cost of wasted meeting time in the UK is 26 billion Euros. It's also not just a problem for higher-level executives, who are said to spend two days of every week in meetings.

Another study estimated that lower-level managers attend on average 12 to 14 meetings a week that take up 20 to 24 hours. As the authors of a great *Harvard Business Review* article about time management problems in the corporate world wrote "Most companies have elaborate procedures for managing capital ... an organization's time, by contrast, goes largely unmanaged." If you become known as someone who knows how to manage it, you will be seen as awesome.

## How to run a meeting in which time flies

In a nutshell, meetings need to be shorter, focused, straightforward, collaborative, integrative, and interactive. Here are my rules.

**Rule # 1: Keep meetings to either 15-20 minutes or if you really need more time, 20-30 minutes**

**Rule #2: Design smaller agendas that focus tightly on one or two specific issues**

Remember the power point slide of a meeting agenda earlier? *Never* write an agenda like that. But do always write an agenda. This will allow you to make sure you don't go into overtime.

Here's an optimal agenda:

- How the heck we got here
  5 mins   Robert Only
- What can we do to fix it
  5 mins   Richie & Robert
- Must make a collective decision
  5 mins   Everyone

**Rule # 3:  Share the agenda before the meeting.**

Just about nothing is more annoying and more of a time-suck in a meeting than people going off-agenda. They're much freer to do that if you haven't made sure 1.) They know there *is* an agenda, and 2.) It makes clear that timing is tight.

**Rule #4: Assign people to lead the discussions of agenda items.**

Create subgroups and or pair members to present on each agenda item, and allot time for each discussion. This way, people are competing for the time; if one group goes over, it's taking away from the others. You'll find the groups will police themselves.

**Rule #5:  Make the discussion collaborative.**

Avoid monologs and a hierarchical structure of authority over the proceedings.   Make it clear that participation is wanted, and expected, from all attendees.

**Rule #6: Get the right people in the room.**

You not only want participation, you want it from the right people. One of the biggest problems with meetings is that the people with first-hand experience of the issues being discussed are so often not invited. This is probably the key reason that so many meetings ramble on and on; most of the attendees have very little understanding of the problems.

Get the people who do in the room and they'll cut to the chase.

**Rule #7: Condone no repetition; no repetition at all, none.**

In almost every meeting I've ever attended (that I didn't run), there's been someone who is fixated on a topic. As soon as someone starts to harp on about something already discussed, swoop in with "we covered that, and as a team we have to move on."

**Rule # 8: Begin and end all meetings on time (or early) regardless of how much or how little is accomplished.**

Punctuality is powerful; it shows the ultimate respect for the time of others. If you stick to this rule, over time you'll find that not only will people love you for it, but that people always show up for your meetings on time, and they will figure out how to get through the agenda in the time allotted.

I have found it better to say, we need to respect everyone's time and schedule a follow up, than to try to cram a complex discussion into five minutes of borrowed time.

One of my favorite meetings happened today as I was driving to the airport on the day I'm writing this page, June 10th 2014. Gary Marshall, who was the CIO at Sungard had left his role, and he was exploring new engaging professional opportunities. Gary and I had spoken about a firm I am on the board of, and we were not sure how he could get involved. But we knew that he was perfect for helping the firm.

Here is the transcript of the call I had with him while I was driving to Newark International Airport in New Jersey.

> R: Gary, I need 10 minutes of your time, this is about XYX company, there've been some promising developments, and I think I have a role for you. It will take a long time to discuss the details, but since we only have 10 mins, how about I tell you what changed, tell you about the role, and then you either say yes or no to the deep dive?

> G: That sounds perfect, I love to have short conversations to decide whether I need the long ones, this is the conversational try-and-buy.

> R: Exactly. Here is what changed. We have a go-to-market company designed to win, stacked with A-players and we need one last piece. I need you for one to two years to be the interim CTO. It will probably take up 10% of your time at a minimum, and 40% of your time at a maximum.

> G: What's in it? For me.

> R: The compensation is equity, it is standard, all of us are using the same formula so that it is simple, transparent and fair.

> G: Hummmm, I like the idea, and if you're telling me you have an A-team that will play nicely, then I am in.

> R: Great. We'll need 1 hour of your time in the next 48 hours. The guys will work out the details. I will let you get back to your day.

> G: Yeah I've got a crap load of other meetings; I wish they could all be 10 mins.

> R: Gary … it's only been five minutes thus far, why don't you take the last five minutes back?

> G: Man I am gonna love working with you!

*While writing this chapter, I listened to
One More Time by Daft Punk*

# INGREDIENT 9:

## *Don't ask for favors, ask for friendship*

L ook around you. How did you end up with the friends you have? I always say, I didn't get a chance to pick my family, so I am definitely going to relish in the opportunity to pick my friends. But I've observed that most often people find their friends – I mean real friends, not Facebook friends – primarily due to proximity.

People become friends with classmates, folks in the neighborhood, colleagues, or friends of friends. I've also noted that people tend to become friends because of the way our friends make us feel. Those we befriend make us feel better about ourselves, because they are supportive, or they laugh at our jokes, or maybe because they are cool and popular, which rubs off on us. The third main reason people become friends is that they share problems; misery loves company.

These are all fine reasons to form friendships. But they're limited. I think most people don't stretch themselves enough and reach out far and wide enough and ask for friendship. If there is one thing that I resented my parents telling me over and over when I was growing up it was "show me your friends and I will tell you who you are." My dad, especially, was adamant that if I kept friends that got into trouble, I would eventually end up in trouble. He was right. Now I get it. The wider and richer a circle of friends you have, the deeper and richer a life you will live and the more successful you will be.

There is so much emphasis in the literature about success on networking and the "culture of reciprocity" of doing favors. If you do someone a favor, you can ask them for a favor. So if favors are so easy, why do so many people dislike networking? Because it's so transactional. Often we only hear from people when they need a favor, and with others, after the favor is granted it's simply thank you and goodbye. Building friendships is by far the better way to go.

## Emailing David Kord Murray

After reading the book *Borrowing Brilliance*, by David Kord Murray, I decided to reach out to him. I liked the way he taught, and, I wanted to be his friend. We lived in different states of the U.S. – him in Colorado and me in New York – and we're two decades apart in age. He's also in a much higher income bracket than me. We weren't going to naturally become friends. Not unless the cosmos interfered.

So I emailed him.

> I simply wrote:
> *Hey David,*
>     *I am just an average middle manager in NYC. I read your book, and it changed my life, and my thinking. Can we be friends?*
> *-R*

It was short, it was to the point, it was heart-felt, and I wasn't asking or a favor. I was asking for friendship. I would have bet heavily against David replying, but the bugger did. We had dinner, with much wine, a few months later in New York (we have divergent recollections of that night; my version is that he couldn't remember what hotel he was staying in after the n+x bottle of wine). Now, five years later we are becoming business partners. If I hadn't sent him that note, I'm sure today I'd just be one of his Twitter followers.

Or more precisely, if I'd sent him a note asking for a favor over friendship, I may never have heard back from him.

## How I got "Aroned"

Sometimes you don't have to ask for friendship, you simply have to be friend-able.

One of my old bosses, a guy who's had a big influence on me and shaped my thinking, called me one day and said, "I want you to meet Aron Dutta, he will change your life." This guy Aron couldn't be cooler. He has driven the Gumball 3000, the annual motor rally that begins in cities like England or Miami and ends in a different city 3,000 miles away every year. He hangs out with rock stars. And his brain has the processing power of a super computer. When he thinks, you can smell brain cells burning.

I ended up working with him on a white paper for the TMForum, a nonprofit focused on helping companies solve the challenges of digital transformation, from cloud management to big data analytics and business process optimization. All of the others working on the paper were A-listers; many with PhDs, people who had registered multiple patents and had grown and taken public several companies. I was by far the gofer boy. Make no mistake about it, if one of these guys wanted coffee, I would go get it.

A few weeks in, I said to Aron "I am severely outgunned, everyone here is so smart, so accomplished. I feel so inadequate even speaking in meetings. How should I deal with this?"

He responded with the single most powerful and memorable sentence anyone has ever said to me.

"NEVER UNDERESTIMATE THE POWER OF A DUMB GUY ASKING QUESTIONS IN A CROWD OF SMART PEOPLE."

I took it to heart, and I stopped worrying about asking questions, and before long, I stopped feeling like the dumb guy. I realized that my questions were more important to the process than my thinking.

Aron and I became friends, and a few years later, I asked him why he had inculcated me into this tribe. He really operates with a "tribe" and he refers to it that way. He answered simply, "I wanted to be your friend."

Building friendships is so much better than doing and asking for favors. The math of favors can get tricky. For one thing, you've got to be sure that you don't ask for favors unless you can repay them. You've also got to carefully calculate how many you ask for and how often. Asking for a favor may seem a whole lot more straightforward and less demanding than asking for friendship. But we all know that often people ask for favors because they think you'll feel obligated and will be reluctant to say no. And it's true that we're reluctant to say no, sometimes because we don't want to divulge that we don't actually have the connection or leverage needed to do the favor, and often because it just feels too socially awkward. See? It's like a form of calculus.

Either way, things are uneasy, and lots of potential longer-term friendships are lost this way. And even with people who do become friends, we've got to be careful about asking too many favors.

Also, if you ask for a favor, that's what you'll get and probably all you'll get, whereas with friendship, people will go the extra mile for you.

Asking for friendship will gain you many favors, but asking for favors will never gain you friendship.

## Friendship and business make a potent cocktail

People often argue that mixing business and friendship is a volatile combo; eventually things will blow up. But consider that many of the most successful companies were started by close friends: Larry Page and Sergey Brin, Steve Jobs and Steve Wozniak, Evan Williams and Biz Stone, Ben Cohen and Jerry Greenfield of Ben & Jerrys, Adam Lowry and Eric Ryan of Method, and on and on. That's not to say that these pairings don't sometimes explode; Mark Zuckerberg and Eduardo Saverin probably don't see a whole lot of one another anymore. But so often, friends who work together to start a business bring a shared passion and a depth of mutual respect and trust that gets them past all of the traumas of launching a company.

Making good friends around the office has been found to greatly increase people's satisfaction in their work. According to a Harvard Business Review article titled "We All Need Friends at Work," a survey by "Gallup found that close work friendships boost employee satisfaction by 50% and people with a best friend at work are seven times more likely to engage fully in their work."

And by making friends with more people outside of your daily work and social sphere, you will discover all sorts of things you may not have gotten word of and build bridges you can cross at some point into new firms or a whole new industry, as I've done moving into the health care space.
But probably the best benefit of making friends in business is that

they bring out the best in us. As an article I enjoyed in FastCompany, titled "Innovation's No-Duh, No-Joke Secret Sauce: Friendship," pointed out: "Among friends, credit is not important; it's the quality of the idea that matters. Egos become irrelevant. The open, honest exchange of ideas that happens when you let your guard down creates better results for everyone."

The trick is to build friendships the right way.

Here is an article I wrote on LinkedIn.com, which shared some of my thoughts on networking and friendship.

## Networking like a Ninja – Seven Skills

I was a nerd in high school.

The type that everyone picked on, even teachers made fun of me, and at the thought of speaking to anyone other than my fellow nerd compatriots I instantaneously perspired. I once fainted in French class during a play rehearsal. Here is how bad it was, my nickname in high school was *"cry baby"*.

Two decades after, my colleagues find me at events holding people by the hands walking them over to meet others, high fiving CEOs I just met, daring people to tweet selfies of them and me, and increasingly folks ask how I did it.

Seemingly, this former cry baby has somehow become some sort of a networking ninja, but when asked for advice I repeatedly come up empty disappointing advice seekers.

So I spent some time taking inventory of these alleged ninja skills, and here they are:

1. **Ask more questions** – (most) people feel good when they talk about themselves, ask five questions before you say anything remotely business like. You should have some generic questions ready, do ivy league colleges still matter, what is the optimal amount of kids a couple should have, or silly things like is kaki a color or a fabric. Your "generic" questions are your awesome sauce and you sprinkle them into the basic questions of where do you work, where do you live, and which college you went to. The ninja skill here is to be **CURIOUS**. People genetically gravitate to people who are curious about them.

2. **Be flirtatious and funny** – I learned this from reading a book called "The Game" (don't ask why I read that book) but I learned about kinetics and laughter. You can touch someone in an impersonal way and build kinetics; a high five for example is a simple way to personalize a meeting. Rarely do high fives get rejected. Laughter releases chemicals that help people fall in love with you (ok I stretched there), but you have to learn to make people laugh. If you have not made someone laugh three times, don't waste time asking for the business card. The ninja skill here is to be **MAG-NETIC**.

3. **Volunteer your clout immediately** – what I learned is that everyone is trying to meet someone. This means that if you volunteer to introduce someone you just met to someone you have known for a long time, you have just demonstrated value. Of course if you are just starting out and you know no one then this is difficult, but you must at a minimum demonstrate the intent to be a valuable contact and willing to share your current or future network. The ninja skill here is to be of **VALUE**.

4. **Say the words "I want to help"** – networking ninjas are the proverbial Mother Theresa of the room. When you meet someone they quickly decide if you are a social parasite, a social climber, a social butterfly, just social, or … someone who likes to help folks. Just say the sentence, *"I don't have that many important contacts, but I want to help folks meet them if they so desire"* and you have just earned networking ninja status. The ninja skill here is to be of **HELP**.

5. **Ask for a friendship not a business card** – too many of us ask for favors before friendships. Friendship is something most of us desire at a deep psychological level. Yet, most of us resist the need to be friends with colleagues. I personally only do business with folks I would consider a friend. Many times this means you have to do "friendly" things together. I make it a habit to deliberately ask to be someone's friend (*"you're too cool man, hey, I'd love to be friends with a guy/gal like you"*) – and that's ninja. When someone is your friend, you guys are past the business card exchange. The ninja skill here is to be **PERSONALBE.**

6. **Share your deepest passion** – I love when I ask someone *"what do you do"* and they say something like *"I rearrange people's teeth for a living"* (dentist), or *"I infect young minds to make the world a better place"* (teacher) – it shows their passion, not their work. Take a moment to show what you are passionate about, I am passionate about *"infecting others with thoughts that builds mental curiosity"* – I'm a ninja in training. The ninja skill here is to be **PASSIONATE** and show it, people aspire to be passionate, or at a minimum gravitate towards passionate personas.

7. **Suggest an experience/outcome for follow-up** – for follow ups ninjas give the person something to look forward to. Here is an example, instead of saying I will reach out to you, you may want to say I will send you that report we talked about, what is your email address? Or, I am in San Francisco in April is there a place you like that I can buy you lunch at, or (my best) I think you are really going to enjoy meeting "John Doe" I will set up a call with both of you guys and make the introduction. The ninja skill here is to be **REMEMBERED**.

If you have not done four of the seven above before you take the business card, move on you have lost the battle.

*While writing this chapter, I listened to*
*Walk This Way by Aerosmith*

# INGREDIENT 10:

## *Pass the buck — never give up the chance to make someone your successor*

You are not truly successful until someone has become your successor. Moving on to new challenges is essential in order to stay at the top of your game; it keeps you sharp and builds your knowledge base and network. Many people used to stay at one corporation for their whole career; these days the average amount of time that people stay at a job is 4.4 years. So moving on is the new normal. But grooming successors for your spot is much less common. Even for CEOs. That's in part because so many CEOs fail so fast, within a couple or three years. But when you think about it, that's only more reason that they should be grooming successors from the start.

Grooming your successors and then facilitating them moving into your spot when you go will be a big advantage to you in a corporate career, and the earlier you begin the better. Just think about the esteem business benefits for Ford CEO Alan Mullaly for not only turning Ford around from the brink of bankruptcy, but for managing such a smooth succession for his protégé, Mark Fields. Not only will you earn respect by grooming your replacement, you will motivate the people working under you to work harder to make them your pick, and, because you assure that someone good is stepping in who can successfully further your accomplishments with your peers and bosses, you will secure the legacy of your accomplishments at the firm in beautiful 360 degrees. Another win, win, win.

## Making sure people don't hate you

Yet another benefit of openly mentoring your successors is that it makes people more forgiving of your ambition, and even of your bluster. As I've made more than clear thus far in this book, I have no self-confidence deficit, and I like to say what I want when I want to. While I've been fortunate that many of my higher-ups and colleagues have either enjoyed or happily tolerated my brashness, some of them have really hated it. I wasn't fully aware of this until my boss's boss at Lehman hit me up the side the head about it after one annual review.

I was twenty-eight, and I'll admit it, I was cocky if not flat out arrogant. I had been made an Assistant Vice President the year before and I told my boss that I thought I deserved to be promoted to Vice President, but he told me there was a policy of a "two year gestation period" before an AVP could be promoted to a VP. I had objected, and that's when my boss's boss called me in to impress upon me that the policy was the policy. To which I responded that I thought the policy was "corporate horseshit," and I asked him whether if Einstein had joined the firm and had been promoted to AVP last year, he would tell Einstein he had to wait two years too. (Remember, I try to get fired once a month.) He replied by saying that while I might like comparing myself to Einstein, I was no Bill Clinton.

Bill Clinton has amazing charisma; off the charts. I'd heard many times that when he walks into a room, everyone feels important, and when I was at a dinner where he spoke, and he walked into the room, that was exactly true. Whether you're a Democrat or Republican, it is hard to not like the guy. You melt in his hands. Monica should be forgiven.

When I talked to my boss about what he had told me, he gave me some great advice. He told me that when I walked into a room, seven out of ten people loved me, but the other three absolutely hated me. "You cannot get promoted like that," he continued. "You are better off if five of ten folks like you a lot — they don't have to love you – and the others don't hate you. At a minimum they need to be able to stand your presence."

That really made an impression on me. I realized that I really had to think about how I was going to go from seven A+s (an A+ is someone that loves me) and three Fs (an F is some that hates me) to five As (an A is someone that only likes me, not love), and five Bs (a B is someone who can at a minimum tolerate me, but doesn't hate me) every time I walked into a room of 10 people.

I talk incredibly fast and I realized this put some people off, so I forced myself to slow my speaking. I started to smile more. I would take the least powerful seat in the room for meetings. I even stopped wearing ties. None of this worked. Three of ten folks still hated me.

Then, around the time I was turning thirty, I heard the phrase "succession planning." I don't remember where, but it really struck me and I studied it. What occurred to me from this was that when you openly plan for your succession, you build the loyalty of those you're grooming and the admiration of your colleagues and higher-ups. I had finally found a mechanism by which I could mitigate people's annoyance with me. I could go back to wearing ties, fast-talking, grabbing the power spot in every room, and only smiling when it came naturally. I'm not saying that my succession planning made the haters into lovers; it just made it much easier for them to tolerate me.

They could see that I wasn't simply hogging success, I was sharing it. I began starting project kickoff meetings by saying "I don't want to be at the helm forever, we are going to start thinking about someone to take my place immediately."

## Letting someone else take the lead

The first time I put this into practice in a highly visible way was when UBS decided to create an enterprise social network. I had been studying social networks for several years, and I was the first person to install social network software for a work group at UBS, first going with Spigit and then moving to BrightIdeas. In the early days I had the technology group, some folks from operations, and a handful of folks from the call centers using social tool to crowd source answers, best practices, and reusable code. I should have started an enterprise social network software firm like Yammer; I'd be flying first class on United now instead of coach on JetBlue. Anyway, by the time the management decided to go company-wide with social, I was the leading candidate for taking the lead on the project, which was highly sought after.

But I turned the role down and suggested that instead I write a white paper on enterprise social networks for the firm and that someone else be given the chance to lead the project. In this way I established myself as the "thought leader" at the company on the topic, and I also became known for being someone who wouldn't hog success.

That white paper on social became the single most impactful piece of writing I've done to change the projectile of my career. It established me as a thought leader, and got me gig after gig speaking at conference after conference, which in turn has led to all sorts of good business outcomes after conference.

# Create your followers

A big part of having awesome sauce in an organization is about being the guy everyone wants to be, wants to follow, and wants to see win. And you cannot win, not long-term, unless everyone wants you to win. In my career, I've learned that an ounce of negativity is worth a pound of support, and that there is no better way to develop followers than to groom others for success.

Succession planning is usually discussed only in terms of CEOs; but you can practice it at any level. Having a great number two you're grooming is one of the best ways to look smart and confident. Bill Clinton has no charm deficit, as I said before, but he also knew how to groom a successor. He often lavished praise on Vice President Al Gore, many times calling him the greatest vice president in history. And Clinton earned a strong boost of support when he picked Gore as his running mate because Gore had been his chief rival and was so widely seen as so smart. (Gore lost the election, of course, and many analysts argued that if he hadn't distanced himself from Clinton in the campaign, he would have won.) Barack Obama also earned kudos by appointing Hilary Clinton to his cabinet, and to such a high profile spot, solidifying her position as front-runner for his successor.

By grooming your replacements, you also stimulate healthy competition among those who work for you, maximizing their performance, and they become your most avid followers. They will also help to shore up your reputation once you leave. Jack Welch famously staged a public competition for his succession among Jeffrey Immelt, James McNerney, Robert Nardelli, and while Immelt prevailed, the others went on to become CEOs of other leading firms, NcNerney at 3M and then Boeing and Nardelli at Home Depot and Chrysler. Welch was widely praised for having groomed three such well-qualified leaders and his reputation as one of the strongest CEOs in American corporate history holds firm. Then there's the sorry saga of Sandy Weill and Citigroup. Weill forced out or held back one after another leading succession contenders, including his right-hand man Jamie Dimon, whom he abruptly fired, and Weill's reputation has been pummeled.

Probably one of the most potentially disastrous successions ever in business was the changing of the guard at Apple, because Steve Jobs was so revered and so widely seen as the driving force that *was*

Apple. But once he learned that his battle with cancer was lost, he stepped back from his duties and moved Tim Cook into clear successorship.

Who would you rather model on Steve Jobs or Sandy Weill?

*While writing this chapter, I listened to*
*When Doves Cry by Prince and The Revolution*

# INGREDIENT 11:

## *Don't be a hero, be Jesus Christ or John Kerry*

One of the reasons that when I was still in my twenties three out of ten people in a room hated me was that I *really* loved being right, especially when I could pummel someone who was wrong.

While this demonstrated that I was somewhat intelligent and knowledgeable, it also demonstrated that I was an asshole.

Take the time I was discussing the language that needed to be in a patent application for a piece of software a team of us were designing at Lehman Brothers. The software created an assembly line for generating reports for customer's monthly and quarterly statements, where each customer's statement can be customized to a very high level of granularity, and created without any human intervention. I was constantly describing the invention to a group of lawyers from a top ten American firm who were working with me on writing the patent application to protect the intellectual property of the invention. We were submitting an XML document as an exhibit to illustrate the innovative nature of the software (no need to know more than that XML is a markup language for web documents, similar to HTML).

One of the lawyers had referred to a piece of coding in the XML document — " " — as a piece of "special character" code when in fact it was what's called a "character entity reference." You don't have to know what either is except to know that while the coding for special characters begins with many different characters, the coding for all character entity references begins with an ampersand. While the two may seem similar, they are two fundamentally different things in XML. Now, for those who don't know XML, the mistake is understandable (to me now). At the time, I went ballistic, because calling a character entity reference a special character was outright wrong. I couldn't help it; the lawyer was a real Don Draper type, in a fancy suit, with, unbelievably, a pocket handkerchief. I had to correct him; and I had a marvelous time doing it.

For fifteen minutes I berated him about the difference between a character entity reference and a special character, and why he should and must understand the difference because it was important to the invention. For good measure I informed him that it was dangerous for him to make assumptions about the inventions of others and that it was his job to ask questions about what he didn't know rather than making assumptions.

I felt I'd been a real hero; I'd saved the patent application and saved the day. I was thrilled with myself. But everyone else in the room thought I was an asshole. The meeting ended not long after. My boss was there and he said to me on the way out of the room, "Boy you really screwed that one up." I was taken aback. I had saved the day! I'd been a hero!! I said, "How's that? I saved us from a mistake." He responded — and I will never forget how his words hit me — "You just gave that law firm the permission to bill us for 500 more hours to go study the difference between a special character and a character entity reference in XML."

So much for being the hero. I spent much time later that night over many glasses of wine reflecting on what I had to do. That's where Jesus Christ came in.

A few years earlier, I was reporting to a great guy, named Bobby Anselmo, one of the best guys I've ever worked for. He isn't just an 5A5B - a guy who; in a room of ten people, is loved by five and tolerated by five - he's a 10A+ with all 10 loving him; I've still never met anyone who didn't love him right away when meeting him. Bobby taught me what leaders consider to be "promotable traits" and helped me understand I had some traits that were the opposite. He also taught me about what he called "conjuring consensus without authority."

The leaders you work for, who have the power to promote you higher and higher and welcome you into the top ranks, don't want you to know how to make people look like idiots by humiliating them with the truth, Bobby told me. They want you to know how to conjure up consensus and then get to the truth. He explained that if you launch into a battle, you may win, but that means the other guy loses, and in business once there is one loser, everyone loses. The only way to win in business is for everyone to win. He summed it up this way: "*Heroes don't get promoted for making other people look wrong, heroes are promoted for making everyone look right, like Jesus Christ.*"

I could see the point, but I hadn't really changed my ways. I *really, really* loved being right. That night over many glasses of vodka this time (better for the head later), I realized just how right he was. I also recalled something my uncle, Mike Singh, told me when I was a late teenager. We were discussing my father, who was an insanely intelligent man but who had no awesome sauce. My mom and dad had divorced not long before, and we were discussing how difficult my dad could be. He always had to be right. Uncle Mike said to me, "Richie, your father taught me a valuable lesson in life, and I want to pass it on to you; he taught me that it is possible for someone to be an educated asshole." Suddenly, I realized that was just what I'd become. You know what they say about apples and trees.

So I decided to change, and I developed a technique for stopping myself from pummeling people with the truth, which I called "The Jesus Christ." Here's how it works.

When I hear someone say something wrong, and my heart starts to race, and I can't wait for a gap of silence so that I can interject and bring out the truth bludgeon, I start counting backwards from 100, and I make myself slow down my breathing. I count and wait, count and wait, controlling my breathing, until someone else picks the fight, and there is always someone else in the room who will do so. Then, to stop myself from barging in on the fight, after it starts I immediately start a new count, from one to ten with the words "one commandment, two commandment…" That reminds me to be Jesus.

Then, to conjure consensus, no matter what's been said in the dispute, and how strongly I feel about the truth, once I get to "ten commandment," I interject this way:

---

"Guys, this is great. It sounds to me like you guys are both saying pretty much the same thing. You're converging on the same conclusion but with some small, important nuances. Why don't we set up some time to keep exploring this further?"

Every time, people have agreed. Every single time.

By practicing this technique, you accomplish many things:

1. You put the nix on an ugly battle of the wits sure to rage on and waste your time;
2. You make both of the folks in the battle look good;
3. Everyone else in the room breaths a sign of relief that you've saved them from enduring yet another such battle; and
4. You become the consensus-builder; you are Jesus Christ.

You can also use the technique on friends and family. I use it all the time outside of work. It even works with kids and complete strangers.

## Flip Flop like John Kerry

Eventually I became so comfortable with not needing to hammer on the truth that I learned the value of a good flip-flop. This is a more counterintuitive technique for consensus building, but if you learn to use it well, it can be very powerful. It involves making a dramatic reversal of a position you've taken.

I used it once in an unpleasant meeting a start-up team I was advising was having with a venture capitalist. Now, I'm no fan of VCs; I like to call them jellyfish people, because the only way a VC can understand your product is if you describe it as a merger of two other products. It's Segway with a Tesla engine. It's Skype plus Instagram. It doesn't matter what you have invented, if you can say to a VC "it's like a merger between jelly and a fish, and we call it jellyfish" you are good for a series A funding round! (VCs hate it when I call them jellyfish people, making it all the more fun.)

Anyway, in this meeting, the VC was being gonzo arrogant and taking advantage of my team because they didn't have the accounting and finance sophistication he had. Of course they didn't; they were building a company; he was counting beans all his life. He was really starting to make them bleed on the fact that they didn't understand

EBIT, pro-forma, pre-smart money, and numerous of the other meaningless buzz words VCs throw around. They started looking to me to defend them and nail this jellyfish, and I was about to, but then I remembered that, in the immortal words of Bobby Anselmo, in business once there is one loser, everyone loses. In this case, I knew if I escalated the situation by defending my team, they wouldn't get the funding. Maybe we'd win the day, but we'd lose the company's future.

So I pulled a John Kerry.

I deserted my team and took the side of the VC. I said "Guys, you are making it difficult for Mr. VC (real name protected). We are supposed to know this stuff. Let's not waste any more of his time. He is clearly willing to do us a favor and invest, but we have to clean our shit up." I then apologized to the VC for our lack of preparedness and for wasting his time, and thanked him for his interest and for his willingness for us to come back when we were better prepared. My team popped a gasket at me after we left.

The VC had never actually said he wanted to invest, and he had not invited us to come back when we had better answers, but I had read the signals that he wanted to offer the funding. I could see that flattering him for being magnanimous would appeal to his enormous ego (his glaring weakness.) I realized that by taking his side, and making ourselves look like asses, my flip would make him flip.

Sure enough, we were able to secure a follow-up meeting, and he committed to a serious A round investment.

What was particularly interesting was that in the follow-up meeting, he didn't even ask us for all of the answers he'd been looking for. He was completely sold from the start.

I've become completely unafraid to pull the John Kerry. I do it without apology and have never had remorse. It's not the right technique for all occasions, but if you pull it in the right moments, with the right people, trust me, it's awesome.

Don't worry on occasion about giving up your allegiance; just don't give your soul.

*While writing this chapter, I listened to*
*You & I (Nobody in the World) by John Legend*

# INGREDIENT 12:

## *Never work for the same person twice, and change industries*

M y first job on Wall Street was working as a software developer for Prudential Securities. It was painful; my introduction to the dreaded work cube. I wrote code, then I wrote more code, and when I was tired, I wrote some more code. I got bored quickly. So in 2002 I quit my job there, walking away from Wall Street work to start a company, License Monitor, with Michael Garvey a police officer, Tom Burger and American Express Financial Adviser, Tom Montagnino a brilliant attorney, and Joseph Watson who was a Notre Dame "Double Domer" – which meant you had two degrees from Notre Dame. Joe was the way into the Annual Notre Dame Business Plan Competition in 2003, and we won the darn thing which exposed us to an avalanche of Venture Capital firms. The company solved a simple problem. The Federal Motor Carrier Safety Association had mandated that trucking and transportation companies check driver records once per year. The spirit of the regulation was to make sure that unsafe or reckless drivers are not driving large trucks carrying potentially hazardous materials. We provided technology with which they could quickly pull up driver records electronically, and we built the equivalent of the FICO score for driver records.

After the successful sale of my position in License Monitor and giving up my role as CIO, I decided to return to the corporate world and I joined Lehman Brothers as Software Development Assistant

Vice President. It was no CIO role, but I loved that I would be able to take what I'd learned from building a startup into a large enterprise. But I discovered that three years is a long time on the Street, and I felt a bit out of place. I had also lost lots of relationship capital I'd built up in my Prudential Securities days prior to License Monitor. But I soon realized this was a good thing. I had been hired because of my expertise in software systems for managing information flow, but to most of those at Lehman, I had no brand. My colleagues and the leadership team had no preconceived notions about me, good or bad! This, I found it to be awesome; and this is because it allowed me to completely reinvent myself.

The conventional wisdom I had been taught was that people travel in tribes in corporate America, and probably nowhere more so than in Wall Street banking. When one of the big bosses leaves one firm for another, he or she usually takes his or her tribe with him or her. So the advice was that throughout your career you should find a tribe and stick with it. I had, surprise, violated the rule when I left banking, and now here I was joining a new tribe in which no one really knew who I was. The advantage of this was that I was carrying no baggage, either from Prudential Securities or from License Monitor.

Reinventing yourself comes in three flavors. What you say and do, who you roll with, and what you don't do. What you say and do, and who you roll with are pretty simple and I will not bore you with the details. I have found however that one of the killer levers to pull when reinventing yourself is in deciding what you do not do. I used my three years at Lehman Brothers to stop being a "tech guy" and become a "business guy."

I achieved this by simply no longer doing technical things. I stopped showing that I had any technical knowledge, and I stopped leading technical conversations. I deliberately dumbed myself out of the brand of being a tech hot shot, and a start-up CIO. By the time I left Lehman, no one remembered I was a tech guy, they all saw me as the brown guy that understands the business.

## Getting out from under an old boss, or why management consultants are always smarter

After having thrived by reinventing myself at Lehman, I made the mistake of leaving the firm to join UBS and work for a gentleman I had worked for eight years prior. To be fair, he had offered me a great job to do some transformational work with hedge funds and private equity, and he'd offered me a killer compensation package. I had also loved working for him that first time. He was smart and witty, he led through constructive criticism, and I had learned a great deal from him. Not everyone felt the same way about working for him. You either loved him or feared him, and more importantly, you were either in his inner circle or out of it. I had been in it.

Of course when I joined him at UBS, I was immediately back in his inner circle, which was one of the appealing features of making the move. With the backing I'd have, I figured the sky would be my limit. Unfortunately, things didn't work out that way. Within the first ninety days I seriously contemplated resigning at least ten times.

You see, my boss (who is still a good friend today) saw me in a certain shape; he was one of those people who think in a square pegs, round holes kind of; there are square holes for which you've got to be a square person and round holes for which you've got to be round person, and you'd better not try to fit into the wrong hole. To work for him, you had to be round, and in the time since I'd last worked for him, I'd become square – well, maybe really more something like a trapezoid:

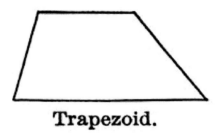

**Trapezoid.**

or a heptagon:

Heptagon

though some might have said I was more like an irregular polygon:

Irregular Polygon

It's true that I was irregular, but that was my strength. Yet my boss at UBS continued to see me just as I had been eight years earlier. He made no recognition of how much I had accomplished in the years since, having started and sold a company, secured two international patents, led teams producing hundreds of millions in revenue, and become known as a popular speaker. He knew about all of that, of course, but it didn't affect how he viewed me. He saw me only as a slightly better version of the guy who had stopped working for him at Prudential Securities eight years ago. We had fun, and I was well paid, but I was severely under employed.

Having learned the value of trying to get fired by pushing for innovation, I started advocating that the bank get into the social space. I wrangled vendors to give me free pilot, vendors such as Spigit and BrightIdeas (early versions of social networks for organizations with a large number of employees), so that I could show my boss and the executive committee how we could build social into UBS. That would allow us to increase collaboration among employees and offer a better customer experience, I told them. I built use cases, drew diagrams, cited the trends, and produced compelling evidence showing how detrimental it would be if we took no action in social. But while my boss heard that I was speaking, he never heard what I was saying.

In his mind, my shape was not that of a strategy guy; I just wasn't the right piece for that hole.

Then he brought in McKinsey to do an executive briefing to recommend ways in which the bank should be investing for growth. Guess what was one of the top three recommendations? Moving into social!

A few weeks later, we launched a social exploration team at the firm, and I led it. But it was ridiculous that it took paying McKinsey to get started. Not only that, but – no offense meant, the McKinsey consultant I worked with on the project was a good guy and we became friends – the McKinsey data was out of date and the projections for social adoption in the enterprise and the descriptions of the science of social and the business outcomes social can bring to large enterprises were about two years behind those I had presented. We could have started a year earlier and gotten out ahead of the pack.

After I launched the social initiative, eighteen months after joining UBS, I started arguing that we needed to attack another problem: mobility. This time we called in Accenture, not McKinsey. And, you've got it, in the top three recommendations Accenture made was going into mobile, and again, what Accenture recommended was two years behind.

No matter what I did in that job, I couldn't change my perceived shape. And this is a widespread problem. Once a boss has a shape of you in mind, it's difficult or impossible to change how they see you.

I am willing to bet that if I were to have dinner with my former UBS boss, now friend, and I asked him about this, he would deny that I had the knowledge and execution chops to have launched the social initiative the year before McKinsey was brought in. But I really can't blame him. I had made the mistake of falling for the lure of joining – in my case rejoining –a tribe and going to work for someone I had worked for before.

Do not ever do that. You will also be stuck in the shape your old boss saw you in, and that will hold you back from growing into your potential to evolve into an always more interesting, multifaceted polyhedron:

Or maybe a great rhombihexacron.

People who cling to a tribe don't truly learn how to fend for themselves, out on their own, and they don't discover all that they're capable of.  Sure, tribes are powerful, and you want to have good relations with a number of them.  But be sure not to drink their Kool-Aid.

## Why I am now in healthcare?

Changing bosses regularly will help you to grow; changing industries will really stretch you.

The End.

CPSIA information can be obtained at www.ICGtesting.com
Printed in the USA
BVOW04*2250031215

428896BV00002B/3/P